D1766750

Delhi in Historical Perspectives

Delhi

in Historical Perspectives

K.A. Nizami

Translated from Urdu by
Ather Farouqui

OXFORD
UNIVERSITY PRESS

OXFORD
UNIVERSITY PRESS

Oxford University Press is a department of the University of Oxford.
It furthers the University's objective of excellence in research, scholarship,
and education by publishing worldwide. Oxford is a registered trademark of
Oxford University Press in the UK and in certain other countries.

Published in India by
Oxford University Press
22 Workspace, 2nd Floor, 1/22 Asaf Ali Road, New Delhi 110 002, India

First Urdu edition published as *Auraq-e musawwar, Ehd-e wusta ki Dilli* in 1972.
Second Urdu edition published as *Dilli tareekh ke aaine mein* in 1989.
First published in English by Oxford University Press in 2020.

ISBN-13 (print edition): 978-0-19-012400-7
ISBN-10 (print edition): 0-19-012400-8

ISBN-13 (eBook): 978-0-19-099190-6
ISBN-10 (eBook): 0-19-099190-9

Typeset in ScalaPro 10/15
by The Graphics Solution, New Delhi 110 092
Printed in India by Rakmo Press, New Delhi 110 020

Contents

....

Translator's Note

....

'Very few cities in the world,' writes Professor Nizami, 'had been a centre of attraction as gorgeous a blaze of glory as Delhi. It was the rich soil of Delhi that accorded it the status of an international city during the medieval period, when diverse Indian cultures flourished there.' *Delhi in Historical Perspectives*, a collection of research papers presented at the University of Delhi and the Ghalib Institute, New Delhi, consists of three chapters: 'Delhi under the Sultanate', 'Delhi under the Mughals', and 'Ghalib's Delhi'.[1] It offers a vivid picture of the chequered history of Delhi, a city where affluence and

---

[1] The book was first published as *Auraq-e musawwar, Ehd-e wusta ki Dilli* (Illustrated Pages: Delhi of Medieval Times) by the Department of Urdu, University of Delhi, in 1972. The second edition of the book, with minor revisions and an additional third chapter, was published as *Dilli tareekh ke aaine mein* (Delhi in Historical Perspectives) by Adam Publishers and Distributers, Delhi, in 1989.

poverty, abstinence and revelry, forts and hutments, and holy shrines and pleasure houses existed side by side. Nizami captures both the brighter and darker aspects of Delhi and its life quite brilliantly. He argues that the people of Delhi constituted a family and were like the beads of a rosary threaded into a string. He aptly quotes celebrated Persian and Urdu poets to substantiate his arguments. His treatment of Ghalib's personality as well as Ghalib's poetry and letters is very sensitive and insightful. He selects stories and events from history to back his narrative and weaves them with the evidence that he gathers from different sources. He imparts freshness and new dimensions to his subject matter with commendable treatment and presentation.

Delhi in Historical Perspectives abounds, like a literary text, in culture-specific words, symbols, metaphors, similes, idiomatic expressions, and other literary devices. These are so embedded in the language of the text that it was quite difficult for me to transplant them in another verbal space and linguistic matrix. The problems that I encountered during the translation of the book concerned lexical and cultural equivalences. In order to negotiate them, I have tried my best to strike a balance between the foreignness and domestication of the target language. In certain footnotes, the information as provided by Nizami in the Urdu original has been retained as is, owing to the difficulty of tracking down the actual sources for more details. The sources of some of the Urdu verses have not been given by Nizami and I have retained this absence on account of their familiarity to Urdu scholars. Similarly, there may be some inconsistencies in the text which have been reproduced by me in the translation.

I owe a deep debt of gratitude to Professor Sharif Husain Qasemi of the University of Delhi, who translated for me the Persian verses and quotes into Urdu.

This was the first book that I picked up for translation towards the end of 2012 and completed by August 2013. Its publication has been delayed for various reasons, and I am happy that it is coming out at a time when people's interest in Delhi, its history, and especially its monuments is unprecedented. I hope that it will serve as a small contribution in this field and will be of help to research scholars and an interesting source of information for general readers.

1

Delhi under the Sultanate

....

In medieval times, Delhi flourished not just as a city but as a cradle of culture and civilization. It was a hub of education and literary accomplishments and a foundry where religious thought, ethics, as well as political and social life were forged. Our common rich cultural heritage evolved in its lap, with the Urdu language being fostered in its environs. The city's chequered history is mired in turbulence as invaders from foreign lands made incessant onslaughts on it. At the same time, it attracted men of wisdom and the arts from far and wide. No city of India could rival the diversity of Delhi's social fabric. Affluence and heart-wrenching poverty, stoic asceticism and ribald revelry existed side by side in this city. Humble thatched shanties existed on the peripheries of magnificent palaces, mighty forts, opulent durbars, and elaborate gardens. Dancing and singing establishments flourished close to mosques and sacred shrines. Its colourful bazaars, *khaneqah*s (tombs of saints; monastery; hospice), madrasas, *serais* (inns), and recreational facilities together presented a picture that could enrapture hearts. The 18th-century poet Mir Taqi Mir captures this aspect of Delhi aptly when he says:

دلی کے نہ تھے کوچے، اوراقِ مُصوّر تھے
جو شکل نظر آئی، تصویر نظر آئی

Delhi's alleyways were the leaves of a painter
Every face that came into sight was but a picture.

Mir, indeed, has drawn a picture of Delhi with such magnificent artistry that it remains etched in our collective memory and constantly reminds us of the glory and effulgence of the Delhi of yore. He has thus sketched a portrait of beauty that lights up the mind and makes us feel as if

یک چراغیست درین خانہ کہ از پر تو آن
ہر کجامی نگری انجمنی ساختہ اند

The house has but one lamp whose effulgence
Lights its every recess, making a spectacle of delight.

Be it the ruins of its palaces, ramparts, or dried up tanks and tombs, together they make a city that still captivates the hearts of tourists. The pages that follow offer a few glimpses of the Delhi of bygone days contextualized with reference to its history.

EARLY HISTORY OF DELHI

The ruins unearthed during the excavations near Purana Qila (Old Fort) just outside Old Delhi bear witness to the antiquity of this city. Archaeologists are of the opinion that the relics of these ruins can be traced to the ancient city of Indraprastha in 1000 BC; in Persian annals, this city is referred to as Inderpat. According to the great Indian epic Mahabharata, the country was initially divided between the feuding cousins—the Kauravas and the Pandavas. After their conflict, Indraprastha came into the possession of the latter, who are said to have built strong fortifications around it with deep moats providing additional protection. Legend has it that the Pandavas had asked the Kauravas to give them five villages, including Inderpat, Baghpat, Tilpat, Sonepat, and Panipat. Obviously, the legend is based on the Mahabharata because four of the villages have been alluded to in the epic, with slightly different names, whereas the fifth one is not mentioned at all. The relics obtained after excavations in these five areas bear witness to their cultural similarity and mutual relationships.

These are the oldest traces we have of the antecedents of Delhi. A more substantiated history of Delhi began in the 11th century when Tomar Rajputs started constructing their palaces in the barren, uninhabited

parts of the Aravali range of mountains. This significant
information regarding the early history of Delhi comes
from an inscription on the Iron Pillar which stands in
the courtyard of Masjid Quwwat-ul-Islam. According
to this inscription, Anangpal of the Tomar Rajputs
founded Delhi between 1053 and 1109 AD. It refers to
Delhi as Dehlu, a name that has endured and resurfaced
at various points of time during its long history. For
example, the 13th-/14th-century poet Amir Khusrau, in
a panegyric to Jalaluddin Khilji, the founder of the Khilji
dynasty of the Delhi Sultanate, writes:

یا یک اسپم بخش، یاز آخور بفرما بارگیر

یا بفرمان ده که که گردوں شنیم و دبلو روم

I may either be rewarded with a horse or may be allowed to select
one from the stable
Or I may be allowed to soar high in the blue and reach Dehlu.

In Persian literature, the first-ever mention of 'Delhi'
can be found in *Safarnama-e Khusrau*.[1] He wrote this
travelogue in the mid-11th century (between 1045 and
1050). However, surprisingly, there is no mention of
Delhi by the great historian Al-Beruni either in *Kitab*
ul-Hind or in *Qanoon-e Masoodi*.

---

[1] *Safarnama-e Khusrau*, Kaviyani Press, Berlin, 1922, p. 67.

Anangpal constructed the oldest city wall around Delhi called Lat Kot, the ruins of which are still visible from the terraces of the Qutub Minar. Amir Khusrau describes the statues of two lions that had chains hanging around their necks and stood flanking the gates of Anangpal's palace. These chains would be pulled by aggrieved subjects to convey their grievances to the ruler.[2] The Moroccan traveller Ibn-e-Batuta, who visited India in 1333, has made a similar observation regarding the palace of Sultan Altamash; perhaps Altamash was inspired by Anangpal.[3] The roads from Qutub to Badarpur and Mehrauli were laid by bringing down the walls of Lat Kot and using the debris as raw material.

The Rajput ruler Prithviraj Chauhan carried out extensions to the structure at Lat Kot. At that time, Delhi did not enjoy the status of capital city. Prithviraj posted his brother, Govind Rai, as the head of the estate. His reign was interrupted by Qutbuddin Aibak's conquest of Delhi in 1192. The latter established a cantonment at Inderpat while retaining his headquarters in Lahore.

[2] Amir Khusrau, *Nau Sipihr*, ed. Waheed Mirza, Calcutta, 1948, p. 244.

[3] Maulvi Mohammad Husain, *Ajaib-ul Asfar* (in Urdu), translated from the original *Rihla*, travelogue by Ibn-e Batuta, Delhi, 1906, p. 53.

Delhi owes its significance in the medieval era to Altamash, who had the foresight to shift his capital from Lahore to Delhi. Thus were laid the foundations of social and cultural institutions which made Delhi or Dilli the heart—*dil*—of India, affording it the sobriquet 'Hazrat-e Dehli' (venerable Delhi). Khusrau called it 'Jannat-e-Adan' (a place in heaven).[4] Osami described its soil as 'Kibriyat-e Ahmar'[5] (brimstone). The Hindus of the Balban era described this prosperous city as 'Dharti Mata' (Mother Earth), with its treasure trove of riches and wealth. This city, as it existed in the medieval era, breathed its last in 1857, when, in the words of Maulana Abul Kalam Azad, 'a city comprising the cemetery of our past life was constructed'.

The story of 'Hazrat-e Dehli' that this writer has set out to narrate is now a forgotten tale of 'Dilli Marhoom' (deceased Dilli). It is interesting as well as salutary. Sir Mohammad Iqbal, the famous Indian poet of Urdu and

[4] In *Qiran-us Sa'dain* (Matba' Nawal Kishore, Lucknow, 1885, p. 22), Khusrau writes: '*Hazrat-e Dehli katf-e din-o daad / Jannat-e Adanat ke abaad baad*' (Hazrat-e Dehli is the sanctuary of religion and justice. It is Jannat-e Aden, may it live long!).

[5] In *Futuh-us Salateen* (A. Mahdi Husain, Agra, 1938, p. 445), Osami writes, '*Chu kibret-e ahmar hama khak-e oo / khirad gashta ajiz idrak-e oo*' (Its land is like an elixir / even intellect fails to penetrate it).

Farsi, saw traces of Delhi in the distant streets of Rome and wrote:

سواد رومۃ الکبر ی میں دلّی یاد آتی ہے

وہی عبرت، وہی عظمت، وہی شان دل آویزی

The Roman avenues bring back memories of Delhi
Admonition, majesty, enchanting grandeur, all are the same.

DELHI: AN URBAN CONGLOMERATE

The medieval city of Delhi did not exist as a single urban entity but was, in fact, a conglomerate of several urban habitats. While the seven cities of Delhi are well known, the real number could be even larger. In *Masalik-ul-Absar*, Abu Bakr Bin Khalal has mentioned as many as 21 cities that made up the city of Delhi. This may be an exaggeration, but there is little doubt that the centre of populated areas did keep shifting from time to time. Ibn-e-Batuta explained that this was because every ruler of Hindustan built a new palace of his own, which the inhabitants gravitated towards, abandoning the old settlements altogether. Obviously, each ruler was guided by his individual notions and geopolitical compulsions, yet this phenomenon of haphazard growth needs to be analysed in the light of the times and particularly in the context of the power wielded by different tribes, impact of continued invasions, changes in the courses of rivers, and economic vicissitudes. Only a few traces of the ancient settlements exist now. It will not be appropriate to attribute the frequent shifts of population to the impact of climatic changes; rather, they can be attributed to the destruction wrought by the rulers themselves. All rulers, including Feroz Shah, Sher Shah, Akbar, and Shahjahan, appropriated existing buildings for their own selfish use, primarily treating them as sources of raw material for constructing their own edifices. More than the shortage of building material, the weakness of human nature was responsible for these desecrations.

Sultan Altamash made Delhi the capital and a centre of cultural confluence. The Hauz-e-Shamsi and Qutub Minar were not merely architectural marvels, in the construction of which both Hindu and Muslim architects were equal partners. More significantly, both structures ushered in a new era of political and cultural fusion that paved the way for an extensive and pluralistic pan-Indian civilizational framework. Altamash turned the capital into the political and cultural nerve centre of the country and rendered it practically impregnable against assaults on its unitary identity. Those who preceded him indeed erected grand palaces and established new hubs for the city's growth. However, none could match the 'sanctity' of Altamash's Daulat Khana: up to the time of Mohammad Bin Tughlaq, every ruler chose the Daulat

Khana as the venue of his coronation ceremony. The coronation ceremony of Altamash had also taken place in the Daulat Khana. The golden crown of the Qutub Minar and the pleasure house of Hauz-i-Shamsi for long remained central features of the city, attracting young and old alike. The sultan constructed a fort that he called Adilabad. He made his people call him 'Adil' (The Just One) and the fort he built was explicitly expressive of this sentiment.

It was the sultan's desire to encompass Delhi, Siri, and Tughlaqabad within a single boundary wall, but his preoccupations with myriad other plans came in the way. Financial constraints, in part, forced him to abandon this grand scheme. He later founded another city, Khurramabad, to commemorate his recognition as King from the Caliph of the day. The surmise that Mohammed bin Tughlaq was responsible for the dismantling of medieval Delhi is far from accurate. However, the centrality of Delhi did suffer a setback during his time and he was responsible for the forced exile of the Sufis from Delhi to Deogiri in the Deccan. The disciples and close aides of Shaikh Nizamuddin Aulia, and the centrality of the Chishti order, were greatly affected by this move.

Feroz Shah Tughlaq laid the foundations of Ferozabad early during his reign. Mutahar, in his inimitable poetic style, observed that perhaps even the legendary painter Mani could not have produced a work of beauty and excellence surpassing Ferozabad's splendour. For about four decades, Ferozabad, located in the area which is now popularly known as Feroz Shah Kotla, remained the capital; of course, at present this area has shrunk beyond recognition. According to Shams Siraj Afeef, the city was dispersed over an area of 10 square miles and it included Inderpat, Sarai Malik Yar Parran, Sarai Shaikh Abu Bakur Tusi, the mausoleum of Razia Sultan, and Mehrauli.[6] People thronged its busy streets and colourful bazaars. Yet it was easy to move about from place to place because of easy availability of various modes of conveyance for hire—*doli*s (palanquins), horses, and bullock carts. A ride in a small cart would cost 4 *jetals*, and in a bullock cart 6 jetals; a horse could be hired for 12 jetals and a doli for half a *tanka*.[7]

These then were the cities built by the sultans of Delhi and the life of ordinary citizens revolved around them. Ibn-e-Batuta noted that the name Dehli was used only for the older part of the city, which was inhabited in the times of the Hindus;[8] the other parts of the city came to be identified by other names.

[6] Shams Siraj Afeef, *Tareekh-e Feroz Shahi of Shams Siraj Afif*, ed. M. Wilayat Husain, Asiatic Society of Bengal, Calcutta, 1891, p. 134.

[7] Afeef, *Tareekh-e Feroz*, p. 136

[8] Husain, *Ajaib-ul Asfar*, vol. II, p. 25.

The city in its entirety was sacked by the Mongol Timur in the year 1398. Even though the Mongol army had often knocked at Delhi's doors, the medieval city had never before faced such loot and plunder. Timur was, however, so greatly impressed by the buildings in Delhi that he took back with him a large number of masons. Who is to say that the buildings in Samarkand do not bear the stamp of the masons of Delhi? Later, Khizr Khan established Khizrabad and Mubarak Shah founded Mubarakpur, but neither city could equal the splendour or political power of its predecessors. An important reason for this was the rise and evolution of provincial centres. As the Lodi sultans of Delhi switched their attention to Agra, Delhi suffered a further setback, not regaining its glory till the era of Shahjehan.

DELHI: AREA, POPULATION, AND GATES

Before turning one's attention to the conditions of life in the urban areas of Delhi, it is of great significance to note that caste played an important role in defining city life during Rajput times. This drawback has been elaborately dealt with in Alberuni's *Kitab-ul Hind* which records that only people of the upper castes were permitted to live within the boundary walls of the city. Lower caste people lived outside of the city limits. The advent of the Turks and their subsequent dominance changed that, and the gates were thrown open to people of all castes. Professor Mohammed Habib has described it as the 'dawn of urban revolution'.[9] The expansion of the cities of the medieval era and the resultant demographic change was an important part of this revolution, leaving a lasting imprint of cosmopolitanism on the character of Delhi. According to Shahabudin Abul Abbas Ahmed, a 14th-century Arab scholar, the city of Delhi was spread over a radius of 40 miles.[10] Amir Khusrau mentioned that both sides of the Jamuna river were inhabited by people. Like the Tigris in Baghdad,[11] the Jamuna flowed through Delhi, splitting it into two parts. Boats of different sizes continuously plied on the river. Afeef writes:

Large boats are afloat in the Yamuna, several of them having space for the storage of 5,000 maunds of foodgrains. Some boats had capacity for even 7,000 maunds, whereas the smaller boats could store up to 2,000 maunds each.[12]

[9] Introduction to vol. II of Henry Elliot and John Dowson, *History of India, as Told by Its Own Historians*, 8 volumes, Aligarh, 1952 [London, 1867–77].

[10] Aḥmad bin'Alī Qalqashandī, *Subh-ul Asha*, in Mohammad Zaki, *Arab Accounts of India in the Fourteenth Century*, Delhi 1981, p. 28.

[11] *Aijaz-e Khusrawi*, Nawal Kishore, Lucknow, vol. II, n.d., pp. 339–40.

[12] Afeef, *Tareekh-e Feroz*, p. 310.

The Ashoka Pillar was carted to Ferozabad on these boats. The expanse of Delhi was indeed vast and its fame had reached far and wide. The much-travelled Ibn-e-Batuta had this to say about Delhi:

The city wall is renowned the world over; its width is about 11 arms' length, being about 17 feet tall. The wall has small rooms, even dwellings for guards and watchmen posted to keep vigil at the city gates. There are stores to stock foodgrains, catapults, and arms. All care is taken to protect the foodstock against damage so that when taken out for consumption there is hardly any change in its freshness. Some rice was taken from these stores in my presence. It had become somewhat dark on the surface, but its taste had not changed. It is said that corn and maize were stocked during Balban's time, 90 years ago. The top of the wall is paved, so that foot soldiers can keep constant watch over the city. The godowns facing the city side have apertures to let the light in. The lower part of the wall is built of stone and the upper part of brick. There are numerous watchtowers standing close to each other.[13]

The number of city *darwazas* (gates) kept increasing and decreasing depending on their use and need. Amir Khusrau, in his *Qiran-us-Sa'dain*, mentions 13 gates and 100 windows.[14] Burni notes that there were 12

[13] Husain, *Ajaib-ul Asfar*, pp. 38–9.
[14] Khusrau, *Qiran-us-Sa'dain*, p. 29.

gates.[15] Timur mentions 10 gates in total,[16] whereas Ibn-e-Batuta writes that there were 28 gates in the city wall. However, there were seven better-known gates of Delhi: Badayun Darwaza, Mandavi Darwaza, Gul Darwaza, Najeeb Darwaza, Karnal Darwaza, Palam Darwaza, and Bajalsa Darwaza.[17] Some annals mention other gates as well. Palam Darwaza was known for its male and female slave markets.[18] Outside Karnal Darwaza were the stables of Delhi,[19] whereas outside Ghazni Darwaza stretched the fields of Eidgah with a graveyard beside it. There were fields beyond Mandvi Darwaza as well, and rows of orchards and gardens covered the vast expanse beyond Gul Darwaza.

Both sides of the roads emerging from the various gates of Delhi and leading to other parts of the country were planted with shady trees. In the times of Mohammad bin Tughlaq, the road from Delhi to

[15] Ziauddin Burni, *Tareekh-e Firoz Shahi*, ed. Saiyid Ahmad Khan, Asiatic Society of Bengal, Calcutta, 1862.

[16] *Malfuzat-e Timuri*, in Elliot and Dowson, *History of India*, vol. III. Timur has counted different doors for different settlements within Delhi, with 13 belonging to the royal palace, 7 to Siri, and 10 to Old Delhi.

[17] Husain, *Ajaib-ul Asfar*, p. 40.

[18] *Jawame-ul Kalem*, p. 13

[19] Syed Mubarak Alavi Kirmani, *Sair-ul Aulia*, Khwaja Hasan Sani Nizami, Delhi, 2000, p. 118.

Deogiri was lined with bushy and shady trees, giving it the appearance of an expansive garden.[20] Milestones were installed at short intervals along the road.[21] Every road from Delhi had outposts known as *alaagh*, which served the purpose of sending and receiving mail. Places where horses were used for carrying the posts were called *aulaq* and places where male messengers carried the posts were called *dawa*.

Normally, the houses in the city were constructed of brick and stone and had wooden roofs. The floors were made of a white stone that looked like white marble. The houses were never higher than two storeys, with most houses being single storeyed. Only the royalty and nobility were allowed to use marble for their palaces.

Muslim nobles and Hindu businessmen and Thakurs had imposing houses while, as Burni notes, high-class Hindus built their houses to resemble royal edifices.

Abundant archaeological remnants of medieval Delhi lie scattered all over its modern-day incarnation in the form of mosques, tombs, towers, tanks, and stepwells. Dilapidated bridges and vestiges of walls belonging to the period are also to be found all over Delhi. A part of Shaikh Nizamuddin Aulia's khaneqah

---

[20] Husain, *Ajaib-ul Asfar*, p. 44.

[21] Husain, *Ajaib-ul Asfar*, p. 167.

is interred near Humayun's tomb. The Ferozi madrasa still exists, but time has battered it beyond recognition. A two-line verse that Sir Syed has used as the title of the second chapter of his book *Aasar-us-Sanadid* comes to mind:

بیاد نقش عمارات شہریاران بین

کہ این سپہر جفا پیشہ چون بہ بست و شکست

Come and witness the relics of the royal palaces to realize
How the cruel hands of the heavens have reduced them to ruins.

CLIMATE OF DELHI

Contrary to the praise they had heard of the climes and environs of Delhi during the medieval period, some chroniclers of the 19th century have noted that they found the climate not very good.[22] Osami has, however, praised it in eloquent terms:

بہ ہر چار فصلش ہواے بہار

ندیدم بہ عمرے چنین مرغزار

Springtime lasts throughout the tetrad of seasons
Never have I witnessed such blossoming in my life.[23]

[22] Sir Syed Ahmed Khan (Bahadur), *Aasar-us Sanadid*, Central Book Depot, Delhi, 1965, p. 457.

[23] Osami, *Futuh-us Salateen*, p. 445.

This praise is indeed greatly exaggerated. Perhaps the climate of Delhi was never pleasant. During the time of Alauddin Khilji, Shaikh Nizamuddin Aulia found the climate around the cantonment area to be better than the climate of Delhi.[24] During the intense heat of summer, water from the wells tasted better than iced water, or water cooled with salt.[25] But the searing heat was a source of extreme discomfort. According to Burni, 'People hang necklaces of onions round the neck to protect themselves against sun stroke.'[26] During Feroz Shah's reign, Delhi's gardens, canals, and *baolis* (stepwells) had a favourable impact on the climate of Delhi, with the hot wind losing its edge. Cultivation, which was severely affected by water shortage, got a boost, but the subsequent closure of canals and levelling of stepwells had an adverse impact. Overpopulation and repeated changes in governments destabilized urban planning, resulting in deterioration in sanitation.

MEDIEVAL DELHI AS A GLOBAL HUB

In the medieval times, Delhi became a global hub and no other city in Asia could rival it. Around this time, when

[24] Amir Hasan Sijzi, *Fawaid-ul Fawad*, Urdu Academy, Delhi, 1990, p. 113 (translated into English by Bruce Lawrence with an introduction by K.A.Nizami, New Jersey, 1992).

[25] Sir Syed, *Aasar-us Sanadid*, p. 203.

[26] Burni, *Tareekh-e Feroz*, p. 570.

Delhi was proclaimed the capital of India, the armies of
Chengiz Khan were moving forward in waves, forcing
many rulers in Central Asia to surrender to them. This
caused a mass exodus of people from Central Asia to
Delhi since their own cultural centres were plundered
by the Mongols. Among these there were, as Osami put
it, innumerable men of letters, tradesmen, and artisans
who crossed over from the Arab lands, Khurasan,
Bukhara, and even China. Osami's poetry highlights
their plight:

رسید ند دروے ز ملک عرب	بسے سیدان صحیح النّسب
بسے نقشبندان اقلیم چیں	بسے کاسبان خراساں زمیں
بسے زابد و عابد از ہر بلاد	بسے عالمان بخارا نژاد
زہر شہر و ہر اصل سیمیں براں	زہر ملک و ہر جنس صنعت گراں
جواہر فروشاں بروں از قیاس	بسے ناقدان جواہر شناس
بسے اہل دانش زہر مرز و بوم	حکیمان یونان، طبیبان روم
چو پروانہ برنور شمع آمدند	دراں شہر فرخندہ جمع آمدند

A loose rendering of the above couplets goes as
follows:

A large number of pedigree Syeds came from Arabia,
So did traders from Khurasan,
Skilled people from China,
Scholars from Bukhara,

Saints and ascetics from several lands,
Artisans of every country,
Beauties from many towns,
Dealers in jewels and jewellery,
Physicians from Greece and Rome,
Intellectuals from everywhere gathered in this noble city
like moths around a candle.[27]

Altamash was able to channelize these talents— variegated, contradictory, and, in some cases, languishing—towards the forging of a cultural and civilizational ethos. Delhi and its hinterland became home to the finest in arts, crafts, and letters from Central Asia and Iran, and the city soon became a surrogate for Baghdad, Bukhara, and Samarkand. Delhi turned into an international city when caravan after caravan started arriving at its doors while Baghdad lost its former glory. Thus, the decline of other centres of Islamic culture gave a boost to Delhi's efflorescence and hardly any other city in Asia could boast as many settlers from outside as Delhi. Balban established as many as 15 localities,[28] where people of different nationalities were

[27] Osami, *Futuh-us Salateen*, pp. 114-15.

[28] *Deebacha Ghurutul Kamal*, National Committee for the 700th Anniversary of Amir Khusrau, Lahore, 1975 (also available in Urdu translation by Lateef Ullah, Scheherezade, Karachi, 2004).

settled. These were named Samarkand, Kashgar, Ghor, Khata, et cetera, after the places of their inhabitants' origin. The global status of Delhi kept rising until it reached its zenith under Alauddin Khilji. Amir Khusrau, Burni, and Osami were eloquent about the scholastic excellence of Delhi; Amir Khusrau with his characteristic flourish declared that a diamond lay hidden underneath every stone in the city. There were poets whose creative talent outshone that of celebrated Arabic poets such as Imara-ul-Qais and Ibn-ul-Jinn.[29] According to Burni, Delhi had scholars of great calibre whose rivals were not to be found even in Bukhara, Samarkand, Baghdad, and Egypt.[30] These scholars were well versed in every branch of Islamic learning, philosophy, logic, and religion. The ulema of Delhi had made it the envy of Baghdad and Egypt, bringing it on a par with Jerusalem.[31] Some were of as great renown as Imam Ghazali and Imam Razi.[32] At a time when the works of the ulema of Samarkand, Khawarizm, and Iraq were regarded as the most authoritative, Osami writes that the writ of the ulema of Delhi ran in Bukhara and Samarkand. People from these two cities would call

[29] *Deebacha Ghurutul Kamal.*

[30] Burni, *Tareekh-e Feroz,* p. 352.

[31] Burni, *Tareekh-e Feroz,* p. 241.

[32] Burni, *Tareekh-e Feroz,* p.353.

on the ulema of Delhi to pronounce *fatwas* (religious verdict) while *mufti*s (experts on Muslim law and scriptures) from there turned to their counterparts in this metropolis for resolution of disputed issues.[33]

The era of Alauddin Khilji was one of close relations between the people of Delhi and Ilkhanis. Khwaja Rasheeduddin Fazlullah, the author of *Jame-ud-Tawarikh*, was accorded a warm welcome when he visited Delhi as an envoy. He was also gifted villages as a token of respect. The income from these villages was sent to him in Basra through visiting traders. Wassaf and the writer of *Masalik-ul-Absar* have also mentioned the names of a few Alkhani envoys. These diplomatic ties led a number of Indian philologists to travel to other countries and vice versa. As mentioned in *Tarikh Ghazan Khan*, Ghazan Khan learned Hindavi and Kashmiri as a result of this cultural exchange and also acquainted himself with the history of India.

India's diplomatic ties grew further during the reign of Mohammed bin Tughlaq, adding to the international repute that Delhi had gradually built, consequently drawing envoys from different Asian and African countries. The opening of missions from East Asia was a special feature of this period. Arabic books such as *Subh-ul Asha*, *Masalik-ul Absar*, *Aldarr-ul Kamnah*, and

---

[33] Osami, *Futuh-us Salateen*, p. 452.

Aleaan-ul Asr mention Delhi with particular regard and if a list of travellers visiting Delhi around this time is prepared, it would reflect the enviable reputation that Delhi had achieved.

After surveying these historical and geographical details, it would be instructive to take a glimpse into the social picture of Delhi; to do so one would have to begin with the khaneqahs, madrasas, serais, and gardens before ultimately reaching the bazaars in and around this great city.

ROYAL PALACES

Almost every successive ruler of Delhi built a palace of his own. The accounts of the era list among these palaces Daulat Khana, Kaushik-e-Ferozi, Qasre-e-Sabz, Qasr-e-Saed, Kaushik-e-Siah, Kaushik-e-La'l, Hazar Sutun, and Farhatabad. From Qutbuddin Aibak to Moizuddin Behram, all made Qasr-e-Safed their place of abode while Allaudin Masood and Nasiruddin Mahmud chose Kaushik-e-Ferozi. The Qasr-e-Sabz was built during the reign of Nasiruddin Mahmud, the last of Altamash's successors; it served as the venue of his historic meeting with Mongol envoys in 1259. This palace stood facing the Badayun Darwaza. Balban built Kaushik-e-La'l during his reign and lived there after being crowned. Jalaluddin Khilji had such a dread of the people's anger against him that he never dared to think of living at Kaushik-e-La'l,[34] but Alauddin lived there during the early part of his reign. Later he converted it into a royal guesthouse.

The decor of the palaces mirrored the tastes and interests of the rulers. Kaiqobad built his palace with red stone and decorated it with silk hangings and golden curtains. Khusrau writes:

اطلس زر بفت بدیوار سنگ

داد بهر سنگ زیا قوت رنگ

Brocades and silks adorn walls of stone,
Each panel a shimmering emerald green.[35]

The ceilings of the palace dazzled the eyes like a mirror would. The sequinned curtains had jewels sewn upon them. According to Ibn-e-Batuta, at the time of the coronation of Mohammed bin Tughlaq, the durbar was studded with countless jewels, including diamonds, and the robes worn for the occasion sparkled so resplendently that the mother of the sultan is said to have lost her eyesight gazing at them.[36] Paintings

---

[34] K.A. Nizami did not give the reason for people's anger.

[35] Khusrau, *Qiran-us Sa'dain*.

[36] Husain, *Ajaib-ul Asfaar*.

of animals and human beings bedecked the walls. However, during the reign of Feroz Shah, paintings on walls and wall hangings were banned.

One had to pass through several gates to reach the royal palace. At the outermost gate sat sentries, pipers, and drummers. Pipes and drums were played at the entry of every emir and, according to Ibn-e-Batuta, the name of the visitor was announced through beats and cadences. There were similar arrangements at the second and third gates. Between the second and third gates, the main proclaimer, Naqeeb-un Naqba, cut a distinguished figure with a turban embellished with golden insignia and peacock feathers and a gold staff in his hand. The other proclaimers had gilded belts around their waists and whips of gold or silver in their hands. At the third gate sat private secretaries to enter the names and arrival and departure timings of the visitors. Every emir could take only a limited number of companions inside with him. It was the duty of one of the sons of the ruler to go through the register after the night's prayers and inform the ruler which emir had been present and which absent. In case any emir absented himself for three days consecutively, he was required to get official approval permitting him fresh entry. Any first-time visitor was obliged to bring along a gift for the sultan. The gifts from emirs were usually lavish and included elephants, horses, and weaponry. *Alims* (learned people) brought the Holy

Quran while dervishes brought prayer mats or *miswak* (a supple twig of a tree used as a toothbrush) as offerings.

When the emperor came and sat on a high throne in the court, proclaimers recited 'Bismillah' (in the name of God) in a loud voice. The emperor often used a big pillow as a back rest and smaller ones were placed at his sides. The vizier remained standing and the clerks stood behind him, with emirs, lawyers, and others further back. The emperor sat resting himself on his shins while a person armed with an elaborate feather fan drove the flies away. Armed sepoys were posted on either side of the emperor and behind them was the line-up of noblemen, theologians, relatives of the king, envoys, and military officers. This was the picture that one would see on entering the durbar.

When Mongol envoys visited the court in the time of Nasiruddin, the Qasr-e Sabz was decorated in a manner that inspired Minhaj us Siraj Juzjani to describe the scene in the following verse:

زترتیب نهاد و رسم واآئین و نشاط او

تو گفتی عرصئہ دہلی بہشت ہشتمیں گشتہ

Everything was neatly arranged and orderly,
Making Delhi an example of the eighth paradise.

The envoys gaped in amazement the sight of the rich flooring, bejewelled tapestry, and gilded livery of the attendants. Minhaj recited his eulogistic poem, one line of which was:

کزیں ترتیب ہندوستان بسے خوشتر ز چیں گشتہ

By virtue of orderliness India looked more beautiful than China.[37]

The pomp and glory of the court grew further under Balban. The golden filigree of the curtains, painted floors, and utensils of gold and silver displayed unparalleled opulence. The echo of loud proclamations could be heard even 2 miles away, sending shivers down one's spine. Royal processions aroused a sense of fear and awe, perhaps deliberately calculated to do so, with wrestlers from Sistan holding menacingly bare and shining swords. Balban's pure white beard on his dazzling sun-like face looked splendid amid the shine and dazzle of the swords.[38] Fazuni Astrabadi noted that the length from the top of Balban's crown to the tip of his beard was 1 yard.[39] Balban's awe-inspiring grandeur

[37] Minhaj us Siraj Juzjani, *Tabqat-e Nasiree*, eds, William Lees and M. Abdul Hai, Calcutta, 1863–4, pp. 317–18.

[38] Burni, *Tareekh-e Feroz*, pp. 5–30.

[39] Mirza Amanullah, *Baheera*, Iran, 1348, p. 12. He writes: 'The Sultan had a long beard, with long face, long crown. The length from the top of his crown to the tip of his beard measured 1 yard.'

presents an intriguing contrast to the decadence that prevailed under his grandson Kaiqobad.

From contemporary accounts, we learn that when Kaiqobad left Delhi to meet his father, Bughra Khan, in Avadh, a bevy of beautiful women kept him company. Adept at singing, the art of repartee, horse-riding, and archery, they made for an explosive combination of beauty, wit, and skill. There was also a batch of comely young boys, a line-up of brides as Burni puts it. Their apparel was studded with diamonds and they wore pearl earrings. They had been so well schooled in the Persian and Indian genres of music that the audience listened to them enthralled. They were an inevitable part of Kaiqobad's contingent. In place of the awe-inspiring loud shouts of the proclaimers and ushers and the boom of guns, the atmosphere reverberated with music and merrymaking. When Bughra Khan saw his son immersed in this dissolute life, he asked him to pledge that he would give up his licentious ways. The son complied for some time, only to soon revert to his old ways. He even refrained from drinking for a few days but his reform was short-lived.

On his return, his hangers-on did their best to draw the sultan back to his life of dissolution and revelry. A comely youth was commissioned to try his charms on Kaiqobad. When the handsome youth came riding a horse on a gold-sequinned black saddle, the guards and the proclaimers too fell for his charm and couldn't muster the courage to stop him. The youth sang in a mellifluous voice:

گر قدم برچشم من خوابی نهاد

دیده بر رہ می نهم تامی روی

If you put your feet against my eyes
I would feign lay out my eyes all along the way you traverse.

The youth then addressed the sultan: 'Master of the world, the opening verse of this ghazal is appropriate for the situation but I dare not recite it before you.' Kaiqobad lost all patience and cut short the rider, asking him to proceed without fear:

سرو سیمینابصحرامی روی

نیک بد عهدی کہ بے مامی روی

Beloved one, you are traversing towards the wilderness
But this is a breach of promise since you are leaving me behind.

Kaiqobad then alighted from his horse and took the youth into his arms in gay abandon. A goblet of wine was offered to the sultan who recited a couplet:

شب زمے تو بہ کنم از بیم ناز شابداں

بامدادان روی ساقی باز درکار آورد

At night I took the oath of abstinence for fear of loved ones,
Only to break it in the morn at the sight of the Saqi, the cup-
bearer.

The sultan was thus once again immersed in his world of dissolute pleasure.

The licentiousness of the ageing Jalaluddin Khilji's court possibly rivalled that of Kaiqobad's. Burni portrayed the scene at his court in vivid terms, comparing its ambience to that of paradise: a moving stream, wave after wave of wine-bearers, slim and maidenly enough to make the devoted and pious alike recant and take to the path of the infidel, put on the sacred thread, and turn the prayer carpet into the sack-cloth of the tavern. Nusrat Bibi and Mehr Afroz belonged to this court; they were acclaimed singers whose fame had spread far and wide and with whom one would fall in love at first sight:

خواستے کہ جان خود را بر سرایشاں نثار کند

He longed to sacrifice his life for him.

Amir Khusrau used to bring a fresh ghazal to the *mehfil* (a gathering) of drunken revelry every night. When Burni started penning his memoirs in his old age, the old images of the beauty and charm of the sweethearts of the court came flooding back. He had retained a vivid memory of everything.

The atmosphere of merrymaking and revelry inevitably spilled over to the populace and, as Burni wrote repeatedly: like ruler, like people. However, it would be wrong to believe that the courts of the Delhi sultans reverberated only with mellifluous music and everyone was immersed in a life of pleasure. The sultans were serious patrons of the arts and learning in the tradition of Altamash. As Minhaj put it, Altamash welcomed the erudite and the saintly with open arms. He used to travel quite a distance in order to receive them.

غالب ظن آن است کہ برگز بادشاہے بحسن اعتقاد و آب دیده و تعظیم علما و مشایخ مثل او از مادر خلقت در قماط سلطنت نیا مده

Probably no other emperor ascended the throne of Delhi who had such deep reverence and respect for scholars and the devout.[40]

The sultan went to receive Shaikh Jalaluddin Tabrezi when the latter reached the outskirts of the city, jumping down from his horse on catching sight of the saint.[41] There is an interesting anecdote about his deep respect for Shaikh Qutbuddin Bakhtiar Kaki. When Khwaja Moinuddin Chishti visited Delhi, he stayed with his disciple Shaikh Qutbuddin Bakhtiar Kaki

---

[40] Minhaj, *Tabqat-e Nasiree*, p. 167.
[41] Jamali, *Sair-ul A'rifeen*, Delhi, 1893, p. 165.

and one day he went to call on his old friend Shaikh-ul-Islam Maulana Najmuddin Sughra. The Maulana, who was busy supervising the construction of a raised platform in the courtyard of his house, gave a rather indifferent welcome to the venerable visitor. The Khwaja commented, 'It seems as if your title of Shaikh-ul-Islam has gone to your head.' To this the Maulana replied, 'I am as sincere to you as I have ever been, but you have chosen such a disciple in this city compared to whom no one seems to care about my being Shaikh-ul-Islam.' Khwaja Ajmeri [another name for Khwaja Moinuddin Chishti] heard this, smiled, and said, 'Don't worry. I shall take Qutbuddin away from Delhi to Ajmer with me.'

As Qutub Saheb set off for Ajmer with his spiritual guide, Altamash followed in his wake along with a throng of people. As Amir Khurd tells us, at every step people picked up the dust off Baba Bakhtiar's feet with great reverence, kissing it and shedding tears. Seeing this spectacle, Khwaja Moinuddin observed: 'Baba Bakhtiar, it would be better for you to remain here, for I don't think disappointing so many hearts is right. Go, I bestow the city into your charge.' The Saint of Ajmer resumed his journey while Altamash happily returned to Delhi with Qutub Saheb.[42]

[42] Kirmani, *Sair-ul Aulia*, pp. 54–5.

According to the historians of that time, Altamash would spend a sum of one crore (perhaps jetal) annually on learning and scholarship.[43] He regularly held debates and discourses in his court.[44] Burni has given detailed accounts of the sermons of Syed Nuruddin Mubarak Ghaznavi. That the sultan obtained books from Baghdad for the education of his children is an indication of the pains he was prepared to take for them to acquire learning.[45] He gave away two villages and one lakh jetal to Khwaja Tajuddin Bukhari for teaching *adab-us salateen* (etiquettes of sultans) to his sons. Famed court poets of this time included Nasri, Ruhani, and Tajuddin Rezah. According to Shaikh Nizamuddin Aulia, the sultan had a sharp memory and could recall verses that he heard just once.[46]

However, this atmosphere of reverence for learning and scholarship did not last under his successors, and it revived only under Balban's rule. Although Balban possessed an exaggerated notion of the status of kingship based on Sassanid ideology, he would still pay visits to the ulema. This was particularly so in the case of Maulana Burhanuddin Balkhi, an eminent scholar of his time.

---

[43] Minhaj, *Tabqat-e Nasiree*, p. 165.

[44] Burni, *Tareekh-e Feroz*, pp. 41–4.

[45] Burni, *Tareekh-e Feroz*, p. 144.

[46] Sijzi, *Fawaid-ul Fawad*, p. 213.

Balkhi was a disciple of Maulana Raziuddin Sana'ni, author of *Mashariq*, as well as Maulana Burhanuddin Marghinani. The sultan paid visits to Balkhi's house.[47] It is reported that once Balban requested Maulana Kamaluddin Zahid, the famous theologian and scholar of Delhi, to accept the post of Shahi Imam. Kamaluddin was none other than the person from whom Shaikh Nizamuddin Aulia received his certificate of proficiency on the Hadith. His reply to Balban was: 'I do not possess anything other than namaz. Does the sultan wish to deprive me of it?' Balban was left with no answer and the Maulana returned home.[48]

There is another interesting anecdote concerning Shaikh Ali Chishti during Balban's rule. Some men came from Chisht to Delhi to take him back home. Balban vanquished them in a verbal duel, quoting a Persian aphorism. This may possibly be an exaggeration but it proves how keen he was to ensure the presence of the saint in Delhi and the esteem in which he held the ulema.

The atmosphere of learning and enlightenment in Delhi further blossomed under Alauddin Khilji, a ruler who did not have any formal education. He undertook far-reaching reforms in society by imposing prohibition

[47] Burni, *Tareekh-e Feroz*, p. 46.
[48] Kirmani, *Sair-ul Aulia*, p. 106.

on wine, curbing malcontents, forcing harlots to enter into marriages, and putting restrictions on soothsayers and peddlers of drugs. On the other hand, he discussed secular policies with Qazi Mughisuddin with such clarity that none of the ulema could gather the courage to dispute his premises.

During Mohammad bin Tughlaq's rule, learning and scholarship were accorded primary importance and scholarly discourses with the ulema were regularly organized. He had a burning thirst for knowledge and also held long confabulations with *jogis* (a hermit, usually Hindu) and Jain savants; talks with the Jain Prabha Suri would continue late into the night. The number of Arabic, Persian, and Hindi poets in his court was estimated to be around one thousand. The process of establishing contact with Hindu savants, as a concerted effort to learn about Hindu philosophy, began during the reign of Mohammed bin Tughlaq.

While discussing the literary and scholarly pursuits of the sultans of Delhi, one of the foremost names is that of Amir Khusrau. His poetic and literary gems belong to the Alai period. Khusrau wrote a rejoinder to Nizamuddin Janjavi's *khamsa* (a five-line stanza), raising the stock of Delhi sky high in the literary world.

Amir Khusrau's personality was many-faceted. His name evokes several images: he is present in a congregation at the khaneqah of Nizamuddin Aulia as a humble disciple; he is going to battle against Tughlaq at the battlefield of Lakhnauti; he is a captive of the Mongols, famished, parched, and with blisters on his feet, but trudging on without a trace of pain on his face; he is reciting his poems at a gathering at the Hauz-e-Shamsi, the audience listening to him enthralled; he is just back from Lakhnauti only to receive the heart-breaking news of the demise of Hazrat Nizamuddin Auliya; he has torn off his apparel and is wallowing in the dust with grief-stricken heart and tears rolling down his cheeks while reciting a befitting two-line verse.

گوری سووے سیج پر، مکھ پر ڈارے کیس

چل خسروَ گھر آپنے، سانجھ بھئی چونھ دیس

The fair damsel is lying on the bed with her hair covering her face
O Khusrau, head for your home as the evening has descended
here.

Amir Khusrau's name recalls several other pleasing images to mind so attractive that one wants to keep recalling them. One can say that they are 'miracles so bewitching that one is irresistibly drawn to them'.

The central facet of Amir Khusrau's philosophy was universalism. He was many different personalities rolled into one. He was at the same time a Sufi, poet, littérateur, maestro of music, royal advisor, and soldier. And he was able to fulfil all these roles to perfection without letting one clash with another. He was able to perceive the play of life from every angle: in the royal court, he was one person; in the khaneqah, where he sat in pursuit of universal truth, he was another. He comprehended the meaning of life and its many attachments, illusions, and deceptions. He observed people of piety who turned their faces away from worldly desires as also those who had wholly immersed themselves in life and were caught in its temptations. He witnessed life in the taverns, and also enjoyed music and festivity. He saw men being slashed in the battlefield just as closely as he witnessed the co-mingling of hearts in the khaneqah. He was privy to the greed and ambition of kings and conquerors but the heartbeat of the hungry and poor echoed in his own heart. Khusrau had been to every nook and cranny of the country: from Lakhnauti to Multan, climbing mountains and crossing rivers, relishing the flora and fauna of the forests, and minutely observing the customs and rituals of the people. All this had endowed him with flexibility of temperament, lofty vision, and tolerance. Thus, he was a defining symbol of cultural Delhi as well as of his age. His enlightened thought represented cultural synthesis and the high values of life in his times. He fully grasped the multifaceted complexities of India's cultural and literary heritage and always saw a place in it for every strand of belief and faith. His love for India was an integral part of his faith.[49] He had an intimate bond with its people, customs, and traditions. He also loved Indian produce. He loved his country more than any other land in the world.[50] Love for Hindustan was the basic building block of his thought and poetry. He extolled Hindustan's climate, natural endowments, people, habits, and customs. According to him:

1. All knowledge sprouted in India to reach the world at large.
2. The people of this country were able to pick up the languages of other countries while others were unable to speak Hindi.
3. People from all over the world came to Hindustan for acquiring knowledge but no Hindu went abroad to do so. Abu Ma'shar came here to receive education and lived in Banaras for 10 years.
4. In the field of mathematics, the discovery of zero was India's achievement.
5. *Kalela wa Dimna*, which was translated into Persian, Arabic, Turkish and Dari, is the picture of Hindustan.

[49] 'If someone asks me in a satirical vein why I love and prefer India, I would say I love it because it is my birthplace. Secondly, the Prophet (PBUH) said: "Love for one's motherland is an integral part of one's faith"' (Khusrau, *Nau Sipihr*, p. 150).

[50] Khusrau, *Nau Sipihr*, pp. 150–91.

6. *Shatranj* (chess) originated in India.
7. The progress made by India in the sphere of music was unparalleled in the world.

It was this love for India that imbued Amir Khusrau's work with a deep tinge of local colour. It was the source of spontaneity and realism in his work and enriched it with patriotic fervour. Khusrau was completely open-minded in religious matters. Not only did he endeavour to understand the Hindu religion sympathetically but he also tried to highlight the parallels between Islam and Hinduism. At one point he bursts out:

نیست هنود ارچه که دیندار چوما

هست هسے جاے باقرار چوما

Hindus may not be as devout in faith as we
But they are like us in daily worldly affairs and matters.[51]

Discussing idol worship in Hinduism, Khusrau wrote that Hindus do not believe that idols represent God in actuality and that:

وانچه که معبود برهمن بفرق

معترف است اوکه نه مثلے است زحق

[51] Khusrau, *Nau Sipihr*, p. 163.

A class of Brahmans believes
in the uniqueness of God with no parallel to Him.[52]

This was the true essence of their faith. According to him:

معترف وحدتو بستی و قدم

قدرت ایجاد بمہ بعد عدم

They believe in the unity of God, in His existence and eternity
And also in His omnipotence to bring back everything to life.[53]

After closely examining the rituals of worship of both Hindus and Muslims, he exhorted Muslims to perceive the element of sincerity in Hindu rituals in these words:

اے کہ ز بت طعنہ بہ ہندو بری

بہ زدے آموز پرستش گری

Those who mock Hindus for idol worship
Need to learn the art of worship from them.

Khusrau's thought thus echoed the precepts and teachings of the great Sufis of his times, emphasizing coexistence and synthesis rather than discord between Islam and Hinduism.

[52] Khusrau, *Nau Sipihr*, p. 165.
[53] Khusrau, *Nau Sipihr*, p. 164.

A similar eclecticism was evident in his approach towards languages and literature. He was well versed in several languages of the land and felt that each had something to recommend it:

گشت چو در علم مقرر سخنم

در سخن بند کنون سگہ زنم

من بزبا نہاے کساں بیشترے

کردہ ام از طبع شنا سا گذرے

دانم و دریافتہ و گفتہ ہم

جستہ و روشن شدہ زاں بیش و کم

Once my arguments have been accepted,
I can say with confidence about India
That I paid attention to other languages
And gathered deep learning,
Having made enquiries, I have declared.
The truth has dawned upon me.

Khusrau said this with reference to Indian languages, expressing the view that what was being said about them was neither notional nor fictional.[54]

In every language, he found a peculiar essence—*namak*, as he called it—imparting it literary potential.

---

[54] Khusrau, *Nau Sipihr*, pp. 172–3.

Thus, he steered clear of linguistic chauvinism. Of the variety of languages spoken in the land, he says:

معبری و گوری و بنگال واود

دبلی و پیرا منش اندر ہمہ حد

این ہمہ ہندویست کہ زایم کہن

عامہ بکار است بہر گونہ سخن

لیک زبانیست دگر کز سخنان

آنست گزیں نزد ہمہ برہمناں

سنسکرت نام ز عہد کہنش

عامہ ندار و خبر ازکن مکنش

ہست دریں عرصہ بہر ناحیتے

مصطلحے خاصہ نہ از عاریتے

سندی و لاہوری و کشمیری و کجر

دھور سمندری و تلنگی و گجر

Each region and each place
Has its own particular terminology originating in its soil:
Sindhi, Lahori, Punjabi, Kashmiri, Kajar,
Dhor, Samundari, Tilangi, Gujari,
Marbi, Ghori, Bengali, Awadhi.
And the languages of Delhi and the surrounding areas
Were all born in India
And are commonly understood and spoken.

> *Yet there is another language*
> *Which in the eyes of Brahmans is the chosen one.*
> *This was known as Sanskrit of ancient times*
> *And most people are not conversant in it.*[55]

He was of the opinion that every language had its own flavour and that it catered to aesthetic needs. One should, therefore, be free of narrow-mindedness and prejudice against other languages.

He was most impressed with the Hindavi language, and wrote about it: ‏از تیغ هندی برّاں تراست‎ (It is sharper than the Indian sword).[56]

He wrote in *Duval Rani-Khizr Khan*:

زبان هندیهم تازی مثال است

کہ آمیزش در انجاکم مجال است

گر آئین عرب نحواست و گرصرف

ازاں آئیندریں کم نیست یک حرف

> *The Indian language (Sanskrit) resembles Arabic.*
> *There is little room for mixture in it.*
> *The Arabs place emphasis on grammar and semantics*
> *And Sanskrit too had this with little room for change in the text.*[57]

---

[55] Khusrau, *Nau Sipihr*, pp. 179–80.

[56] *Aijaz-e Khusrawi*, pp. 177–8.

[57] Amir Khusrau, *Duval Rani-Khizr Khan*, corrected by Maulana Rasheed Ahmad Salim, Aligarh, 1917, p. 42.

He asserted that Hindavi was in no way inferior to Persian:

غلط کردم گر از دانش زنی دم

نہلفظ ہندویست از پارسی کم

I have erred, if I told you that
Hindi is in any way inferior to Persian.[58]

It was his ardent desire to bring Persian closer to the Indian languages and thus he favoured minimal use of Arabic words.[59] This point has been brought out in *Afsana-e-Shahaan* with reference to the qualities of Khusrau's poetry.

Muhammad Kabir writes that Amir Khusrau has used Hindi words in his poetry in a way that makes it difficult to differentiate them from Persian.[60]

درمیان اشعار امیر خسرو الفاظ ہندی چنان درج کرده است کہ ہیچ کس درفارسی و ہندی فرق کردن نتوانست

Khusrau did not think that it was appropriate to write Arabic and Persian words without diacritical marks

[58] Khusrau, *Duval Rani-Khizr Khan*, p. 41.

[59] *Aijaz-e Khusrawi*, vol. I, pp. 84–5, 90.

[60] Muhammad Kabir, *Afsana-e-Shahaan*, B.M.Ms Add. 24409, p. 37.

which, he felt, deprived many readers of depth as well as finesse.[61] He fixed nine modes of expressions in Persian prose.[62] He identified the seventh mode to be that of the laymen and the eighth of traders. It shows that he acknowledged the contributions of laymen as well as of the trading classes to the evolution of the language.

DELHI'S *KHANEQAHS*

Khaneqahs formed an important part of Delhi's social life in medieval times. As recorded in *Subh-ul Asha*, there were two thousand khaneqahs during the reign of Mohammed bin Tughlaq. These Sufi abodes served different purposes. There were shades of difference in their ambience and the arrangement of their *jamaat khana* (assembly chambers), lodgings, and structures. People of all faiths, classes, and genders frequented these hallowed spots and Hindavi was usually the language spoken at the congregations. The Sufis steered clear of durbars, which they regarded as being contrary to a spiritual ethos.

The established Sufi orders in the country, particularly the Chishtia and Suhrawardia, were founded in India at the time of the Delhi Sultanate and,

---

[61] *Aijaz-e Khusrawi*, vol. I, p. 82.

[62] Aijaz-e Khusrawi, vol. I, pp. 53–4.

within the span of a century, a countrywide network
of khaneqahs was established. The khaneqahs of
Suhrawardia saints such as Qazi Hamiduddin Nagori,
Shaikh Jalaluddin Tabrezi, and Shaikh Ziauddin Rumi
were indeed established in Delhi, but most of the Delhi
khaneqahs were of saints of the Chishtia order. Sufis of
the Firdausi order also settled in Delhi for a brief period
of time. As the climate did not seem to be conducive
for the growth of this order, they moved on to Bihar.
Another denomination of Sufi saints in Delhi was the
Haideris led by Syed Abu Bakr Haideri Toosi Qalandari.
The Haideris had iron chains hanging around their
necks and wore distinctive wristbands. They also kept
sharp knives with them. Close to the Toosi abode was
the khaneqah of Malik Yar Parran, who belonged to the
Ishaqia order. Its followers were garbed in yellow and
carried flags of the same colour.

The Sufis of Delhi held social unification to be their
mission. They stressed the need for a common language
of the people to create stronger bonds among them.
This led to the evolution of a language of the masses
integrating elements from different tongues. A close
study of the writings of some Sufis reveals that they have
liberally used Hindustani words, idioms, and proverbs,
integrating them well with Persian. Words such as *khat*
(sour), *khichri* (a dish with rice and lentils), *matka* (an
earthen pot), *mondha* (a stool made of reeds), and *dola*

(a palanquin), which were all part of everyday parlance, became integrated in the vocabulary of Delhi's Sufis. Thus, there was an instantly recognizable element of the Hindustani way of living in their everyday lives. For instance, the word *beta* (son) was frequently used instead of *pisar*, *bhai* (brother) instead of *braather*, and *mai* (mother) instead of *maader*. Poems in Hindustani were also recited at the khaneqahs and it has been recorded that once Sheikh Nizamuddin Aulia was completely beside himself after listening to some Hindustani verses, reaching an ecstatic state of spiritual joy.

Khaneqahs were governed by a meticulously laid-down regimen of rules, regulations, orderliness, and discipline, which extended also to the enrolment of disciples. Disciples in the higher order were required to shave their heads, or as it was commonly known, become *mahluk*. At the time of swearing allegiance to the spiritual guide, they had to take a pledge to abstain from the sins of the heart, hands, and eyes and were given miswaks as a symbol of physical cleanliness. *Samaa* (spiritual music) was an entrenched feature of khaneqah life in Delhi. It was introduced in Delhi at the initiative of Qazi Minhaj, Qazi Hamiduddin Nagori, and Qutub Saheb. Once in the course of a samaa in the khaneqah of Sheikh Ali Sijzi, where Qutub Saheb was also present, the qawwal sang the following verse by Ahmad-e-Jam.

کشتگان خنجر تسلیم را

بر زماں از عیب جانے دیگر است

The one who lays down his life following the blow of a sword
Gets a new life from God.

The verse sent Qutub Saheb into a trance that
lasted for four days. On the fifth day, while still in
a state of trance, he left this world for his heavenly
abode. Thereafter, samaa became the regular practice
in khaneqahs. The sultans, under the influence of the
ulema, tried to prohibit the holding of samaa forthwith,
but they were unsuccessful.

One of most respected khaneqahs of Delhi during the
medieval period was that of Hazrat Nizamuddin Aulia.
It was in the hamlet of Ghiaspur, adjacent to where
Humayun's Tomb is situated today, a few miles from
Siri in Delhi which was colonized by Alauddin Khilji.
The Jamuna flowed by it. A many-pillared big hall,
which was called jamaat khana, was the central part of
the khaneqah. There were smaller rooms on both sides
and a large banyan tree lent its shade over the front yard.
Verandas surrounded the yard and in some places there
were raised walls for separate chambers. At the threshold
of the jamaat khana were doors opening on both sides,
serving as the main entrance. Adjoining was the *langar
khana,* the free public kitchen. The threshold was big

enough to accommodate a large number of people at any given time. The room above the jamaat khana had wooden walls. Shaikh Nizamuddin Aulia lived in this room. The rooftop was ringed by low walls that were slightly higher at the spot where Shaikh Nizamuddin Aulia sat propped against the wall and addressed his disciples. He would come downstairs and sit in the jamaat khana to meet and address the common people. During summer noons, the Shaikh stayed in a small room in the jamaat khana.

The khaneqah was filled with visitors from morning till late at night. Ghiaspur was located some distance away from the city but the road was always full of people as if they were going to a *mela* (fair or carnival). According to Burni, many people had erected improvised thatched structures all along the road from the city to Ghiaspur with sacks covering the ground. People rested there, drank water, and said their prayers before heading to the jamaat khana.

Shaikh Fariduddin Ganj Shakar, the spiritual guide of Shaikh Nizamuddin Aulia, had blessed him that he would live like a leafy tree, sheltering and comforting people. During the medieval period in Delhi, he was indeed like a tree, spreading its shade over thousands of troubled hearts and minds who found solace in his khaneqah. He gave a patient hearing to all aggrieved souls and encouraged them to persevere patiently in the trials and tribulations of life. The devotees brought all kinds of gifts for him. He took the gifts only to distribute them among the needy, retaining and hoarding nothing in the jamaat khana. Thousands of people ate their fill in the free public kitchen. But fasting was an integral part of the Shaikh's routine. He ate little and his diet included a small quantity of vegetables with a piece of bread. When he was asked to take his *sehari* (pre-dawn meal), tears would well up in his eyes as he remembered people who could not afford any meals at all. He would say that there were several starving people lying in the corners of mosques or wandering here and there, adding that he did not feel like eating under such circumstances.

One day he was taking a walk along the banks of the Jamuna when he saw an old woman pulling water from a well. He stopped and asked her the reason for exerting herself when the river was so close by. The woman replied that she was very poor and the river water helped the food digest too easily, making her feel hungry again too soon. The Shaikh was so moved by this reply that he could not contain his tears and later undertook the responsibility of bearing her household expenses. Once during the hot summer months, a number of thatched huts in Ghiaspur caught fire. The Shaikh went upstairs and paced barefoot up and down until the fire was put out. He later called his servant Iqbal to count the number of burnt houses. For interim relief, he sent each of them some money, food, and cold water.

The Shaikh remained away from sultans and courtiers and also from worldly affairs. He advised his disciples:

بردر شاہاں نروی وصلہ شاہاں نگیری

Do not venture near kings, nor seek their rich offerings.

The above sentence can also be found in the prescription that he offered to his disciples. Despite this, Ghiasuddin Tughlaq, influenced by some ulema, was somewhat angry with the Shaikh. He sent him a command that he should leave Delhi before Ghiasuddin's return from the Lakhnauti expedition.[63] The saint's famous reply was: '*Hunoz Dilli door ast*' (Delhi is still far away.) The sultan was not destined to return to Delhi alive. It was his dead body that came to Delhi. The saint's reply became a proverb thereafter.

The Shaikh regarded selfless service to the people as synonymous with religion. He believed that the spirit of faith consisted of two kinds of worship: obligatory and

[63] In 1323–4, as a response to the request by nobles of Firuz Shah, the independent ruler of Lakhnauti, Ghiasuddin marched into Bengal. In the ensuing battle, the Bengal ruler was defeated. On his way back from Bengal, Ghiasuddin also defeated the Raja of Tirhut in north Bihar.

non-obligatory. The former included fasting, namaz, and Hajj, prescribed for individual benefit, while the latter consisted of acts and deeds for the welfare of humankind. Importantly enough, the latter was rated by the Shaikh as a higher order of worship. Indeed, the Shaikh believed in the innate goodness of human beings and in this scheme of things people were required to do good even if somebody wished them ill. He said, 'If someone puts thorns in one's way, and the other person also does the same in response, the world will turn into a place full of thorns.' Although it is human nature to repay goodness with goodness and evil with evil, the saint never sought to harm even those who had done ill by him.

The saint consistently sought to establish good relations and cordiality between different sections of people on ethical and humanistic grounds, on principles, not on the basis of social or political expediency. He believed in the oneness of humanity, as also in the fact that all the creatures on this earth are from the family of Allah. He wanted no one to be discriminated against on the basis of faith and creed. No wonder he drew Hindu and Muslim devotees in equal numbers. The Jamuna flowed near his khaneqah. Hindu devotees too came to his khaneqah, sang their hymns to God, played music, and offered ritual worship. One fine morning, when the Shaikh was strolling on the rooftop of the jamaat khana, he caught sight of his Hindu devotees worshipping idols. He promptly said:

بر قوم راست راہے دینے و قبلہ گاہے

Each community has a righteous path, faith, and mode of worship.

This sentence eloquently reflects his way of thinking as well as the basic principles governing the khaneqah order that shaped the social life of medieval Delhi.

FEROZI MADRASA

گفت این جای چہ جائیست بدیں زینت و زیب

باز این باغ چہ باغست ز انواع شمار

گفتم این مدرسہ و باغ شہنشاہ جہانست

اندرون آئی کہ یک حُسن بہ بینی بہ ہزار

He said: What a place it is! So well-decorated, so attractive.
Which type of garden? What should it be named after?
I said: This garden and madrasa belong to the king of the world
Enter it, you will witness thousands of merits, enchanting beauties.

From the khaneqah of Shaikh Saheb, let us now move to another important institution: the madrasa (seminary). During the 14th century, there were one thousand madrasas in Delhi. This count gives an idea of the atmosphere of learning and scholarly engagement in the city. The expenses of some madrasas were borne by the rulers and of some by the nobles. Those madrasas that did not depend on help from the sultans and nobles had a paucity of funds. However, the teachers in these madrasas were all men of fame, attracting students from far and wide. The Ferozi Madrasa was the most distinguished institution during medieval times. It was situated in the southern corner of Hauz Khas at the site where Tughlaq Shah fought the historic battle that established the rule of his dynasty. Feroz Shah founded the madrasa in 1352. Its ambience and climate found favour with the people and they built houses nearby, turning the neighbourhood into a madrasa town. Burni described this new hamlet that was founded around the madrasa as follows:

''مقیماں شہر از شیفتگی ہواۓ جان ربائی مدرسہ اوطان قدیم را ترک می

آرند و درجوار مدرسہ مذکور خانہ ہا می سازند''

The inhabitants of the city have started abandoning their old houses and, allured by this madrasa, are settling around it.

The Ferozi Madrasa was a two-storey building. The upper storey had arched verandas and the windows opened out to balconies that jutted out. The entire edifice was a charming synthesis of Hindu pillars and Muslim arches. It was surrounded by a sprawling garden with greenery and flowers in abundance. Poet Mathar, hailing from Katra, once visited Delhi with his friends. As he stepped into the premises of the madrasa, he was completely enchanted by the sight of its garden full of a variety of fragrant flowers such as hyacinths, roses, and tulips. In the middle stood the madrasa with its yellow sandstone walls glinting like a mirror and the reflection of the sun in the water bewitching the eye. The madrasa had separate rooms for teachers and students. The guest rooms were expensively and tastefully decorated with woven carpets brought from far-off places such as Shiraz, Yemen, and Damascus. The teachers of the madrasa wore gowns and their headgear was brought from Egypt and Syria.

عالمان عربی لفظ و عراقی دانش

بمه درجبئه شامی وبه مصری دستار

Learned in Iraqi wisdom and fluent in Arabic language, the savants
would don turbans of Egypt and gowns of the Levant.

The state afforded them rich food, which included fish and fowl, fruit, and halwa of high quality. The madrasa paid special attention to the hostel facilities. A perfect relationship of harmony prevailed between the teachers and the students. Invariably, the head teacher was a person of prominence and an embodiment of knowledge. Maulana Jaluddin Rumi, for example, had mastery over 14 disciplines of philosophy and science. An interactive method of teaching was adopted in the madrasa. For the realization of the goals of education, as also for the reinforcement of classroom interactions, debates were held with students so that they could understand the finer points of knowledge.

هم چناں یک دگر از طالب علماں ہر سوئے

بر فلک بردہ صدا غلغل بحث و تکرار

This way everywhere the pupils are revising their lessons and scholars are busy debating.
It seems as if their voices are tearing through the sky.

TANKS AND *BAOLIS* OF DELHI

Medieval Delhi boasted a large network of tanks, wells, and baolis. Different means were employed for carrying water from one place to another. Centuries later, two visiting experts from Japan published photos of the remnants of devices used for transporting water in Delhi during medieval times, showing how it was dealing effectively with water shortage. Water was obviously an extremely crucial requirement and social life revolved around *hauzes* (water tanks). Altamash had Hauz-e-

Shamsi built between two hillocks, with its waves lapping against the foot of the hillocks. The hauz got its water from the Jamuna through canals, creating a reservoir for fresh water supply to the entire town. A raised platform and a high building was built in the middle of the hauz.

In a sense, the cultural life of the city revolved around this hauz. There were chambers built for Sufis to give lessons in asceticism. Similarly, nestling among the hillocks were tents pegged by people for entertainment and merrymaking. Khusrau has noted:

گردوے از اہل تماشا گروہ

دامن خیمہشدہ دامان کوہ

Groups of merry revellers dancing in circles
Are tucked into tents in the lap of the mountains.

Symposia of poetry were a regular feature of this life where poets recited their verses amid applause. Khusrau was overcome by nostalgia for Hauz-e-Shamsi while away in Avadh in the company of Kaiqobad, and wrote a letter in verse to his friend Tajuddin Zahid conveying his feelings:

با یاد تو در خیال بازی	شبہا من و دل بغم نوازی
صد جانے درونہ داغ گشتہ	دل سوختہ چوں چراغ گشتہ
آبے و ہزار تیر دل دوز	دروے و ہزار آہ جاں سوز
دل درطرب و نشاط بستن	کو آں بوفا بہم نشستن

گہ دادن درّ نظم چوں نوش   از درج دہن بحلقہ گوش

گاہے ببدیہہ دل آویز   سفتن گہرے بخامہ تیز

گاہے غزلے جواب گفتن   گاہے سخن شراب گفتن

گہ جام نشاط نوش کردن   گہ زخمہ تر بگوش کردن

گہ کردن گشت سوئے بستاں   گاہے بطواف حوض سلطاں

شب روز کنم ز آہ جانسوز   زیں گونہ بود شب مرا روز

Loneliness was around during the night
And there was I and the pain of separation.
Now I spend my time remembering you;
My heart is snuffed out like a candle
Riddled with holes
Thousand sighs escape my lips
Like the shafts of an arrow.
Gone are the days of our being together
Loving each other,
No more the pleasure or happiness of your company,
Nor hearing pearls of sweet poetry
Flowing from your mouth, soothing to my ears,
At times penning pearls of words myself,
Spinning out a ghazal in reply to yours,
Talking of wine and drinking,
Strolling in the garden green,
Endless walks along the Sultani Hauz.
Now what remains for me are sighs
And spending days and nights this way.

Another story relating to Hauz-e-Shamsi reveals the reverence people had for Nizamuddin Aulia. One day, Amir Hasan Ala Sijzi was drinking with his friend near Hauz-e-Shamsi when Shaikh Nizamuddin Aulia happened to pass by. The Shaikh had known him since his days in Badayun. Amir Hasan, in a moment of levity, recited two rather cheeky verses to the Shaikh:

سالہا باشد کہ ماہم صحبتیم

گرز صحبتہا اثر بودے کجاست

زبدتاں فسق ازدل ماکم کرد

فسق مایاں بہبتر از زبد شماست

We have been keeping each other's company for years
And if keeping company could make a difference
Then why has your asceticism not done anything to lessen my
transgressions. Thus my transgressions are better than your
piety.

The Shaikh looked up hearing the remarks and uttered, 'The company one keeps does wield its influence.' These words hit Sijzi like an arrow. He fell at the feet of the Shaikh recanting with a verse:

اے حسن تو بہ آنگہے کردی

کہ ترا قوت گناہ نماند

O Beauty, you turned to repentance and abandoned sinful ways
You did so for you were left with no strength, no power to indulge
in sins.

THE ECONOMY

Subh-ul Asha mentions many big and small bazaars in medieval Delhi, filled with goods from other lands of Asia, including textiles from China, Iraq, and Alexandria.[64] The shops did brisk business. The people seemed to be rolling in wealth. Khusrau wrote: 'There flows a golden canal in the city's *dareeban* (betel market).'[65]

A large number of foreign traders had come and settled in the Delhi of those times and they were invariably called Khurasanis. During the reign of Mohammad bin Tughlaq, Yahya Sirhindi recalls that traders had built imposing buildings for themselves and their businesses had spread far and wide.[66] Khusrau complained about their coming to Delhi. He wrote that the traders had come to Delhi after making a lot of money from Sham, Habsh, Misr, and Madain.

[64] Qalqashandī, *Subh-ul Asha*, p. 51.

[65] *Aijaz-e Khusrawi*, vol. II, p. 319.

[66] Yahya Sirhindi, *Tareekh-e Mubarak Shahi*, ed. Mohammad Hidayat Husain, Calcutta, 1931, pp. 107–8.

اکنوں سوے دہلی کہ سواد اعظم است تا ایں سواد را نیز باہمہ
ہندوستان بشویند و بردند

*Now they have come to Delhi where they can rob it of all its
wealth and then go back to their own lands.*[67]

Delhi's moneylenders, or mahajans, most of whom
were Hindus, lent money to the nobles at exorbitant
interest rates of 10 per cent a year or even higher.[68] They
also lent money to local traders at slightly lower rates.
According to Burni, the moneylenders were a highly
respected group of people. They wore brocade dresses
and moved about the city on horseback. Usually they
had Muslim servants.

Delhi had a large number of craftsmen, particularly
during the days of Alauddin Khilji. The *Tareekh-e-Feroz
Shahi* mentions:

آنچناں صنعت گراں ہنر مند و پیشہ وران مابر شہر دہلی را وقتے یاد
نبودہ است۔

*I wonder how Delhi had such accomplished artisans and
craftsmen.*[69]

---

[67] *Aijaz-e Khusrawi*, vol. II, p. 319.

[68] *Aijaz-e Khusrawi*, vol. II, p. 319.

[69] Burni, *Tareekh-e Feroz*, p. 365.

Delhi's craftsmen were skilled in their trades, especially tailors and others engaged in making apparel. They were identified by their trade names. Khusrau wrote about the artisans of Delhi:

ہر چہ ز صنعت بہمہ عالم است

ہست در ایشان و زیادت ہم است

They are well versed in all the crafts of the world,
Perhaps they know much more than that.[70]

We can get some idea of the prosperity of the city from the fact that there were four thousand artisans engaged in the manufacture of silk cloth alone. As a rule, royal palaces had shops and manufacturing units within their own premises, although the units purchased certain necessary things from outside as well. During Feroz Shah's rule, as many as thirty-six manufacturing units were located inside the fort and each was under the care of an emir. Their wares were classified into *ratibi* (perishable) and *ghair-ratibi* (non-perishable).

A most comprehensive and absorbing account of the bazaars of Delhi during Alauddin Khilji's reign is available in the *Tareekh-e Firoz Shahi*. The biggest achievement of the sultan was that he brought rising

[70] Khusrau, *Qiran-us Sa'dain*, p. 34.

prices under control and banned the hoarding of foodgrains. High costs of living and rampant alcoholism were the banes of society as were anti-social elements. Alauddin dealt with these problems with a stern hand and he even forcibly brought hidden money into circulation, not sparing the upper classes and religious trusts in his quest to restore economic balance. He fixed prices in order to put an end to black marketeering and hoarding, bringing cities and bazaars as well as villages under the ambit. His officers ensured an integrated approach, covering both urban and rural areas. The policy proved to be an outstanding success.

The sultan set up the Sarai Adl (Court of Justice) in the open ground in front of the Badayun Darwaza, and stores for selling wholesale goods too were established there. Any trader hoarding goods at home was liable to have his entire stock confiscated. The Sarai Adl opened early in the morning and remained open till afternoon. Traders were required to register their names with the state while prices were fixed by the durbar. In case of shortages, the sultan would arrange money from the treasury and purchase articles through his own men. A permit system was introduced for certain purchases— for instance, high-quality clothing—of which Burni wrote:

"تارئیس پروانہ ند بدوکاغذے بایشان خود ننویسد از سرائے عدل ندہند۔

They should not be given anything from the court unless there is a permit from Sarai Adl in writing.[71]

The prices of all edible commodities, textile goods, livestock, and slaves, even of *rewdi* (a low-cost sweet) and combs, had been fixed, as Burni has revealed. No one dared charge even a jetal more. An effective spy system was operational to enforce the fixed price, with even small boys employed to keep an eye on buying and selling in the market; at times they would themselves take part in buying and selling. Thus, the sultan managed to keep himself informed regarding trade activities in his land, so much so that the people started attributing to him the power to perform miracles. Goods sold in the marketplace were affordable, with wheat being sold at seven and a half jetals per maund, barley at four jetals, rice at five jetals, mash at five jetals per maund, *misri* (sugar candy) at two and a half jetals per *seer* (a measure of weight, about 2 pounds), gram at five and a half jetals per maund, *moth* (a kind of pulse) at three jetals per maund, sugar candy at two and a half jetals per seer, salt at five and a half jetals per maund, and ghee and oil at one jetal a seer each. The reduced prices came as a great relief to the common populace. Even a beggar was able to afford a couple of quilts. One quilt could

[71] Burni, *Tareekh-e Firoz*, p. 311.

be procured in a few jetals. Two tankas sufficed to treat a friend to a hearty meal. A good many public kitchens sprouted up in the city, such as the langar of Ramzan Qalandar and Malik Yar Parran. They operated round the clock. During the month of Safar, public kitchens were arranged in orchards, at tanks' edges, and by the wayside. As Syed Mohammad Gesu Daraz put it, for two tankas, parents were able to buy the goods to give to their daughters a dowry.

بدو تنکہ نقرہ دراں ایّام از جہیزے غم می گشتند بلکہ چیزے فاضل
ماندے۔ (جوا مع الکلم)

In those days, merely two tankas sufficed for dowry, one could even save from that amount.

Once, Qazi Hamiuddin, a confidant of the sultan and the keeper of the fort, explained the aims and objectives of the sultan to Hazrat Naseeruddin Chiragh-e Dilli while narrating the following incident:

Once I found Sultan Alauddin sitting on the throne, lost in thought, his head bare. Hitting the floor with his feet, so lost was he that he did not notice my presence when I approached him. Then I returned and narrated the matter to Malik Qarabeg and asked him to come along with me to see the situation for himself. After this, I decided to go back to the sultan and this time I gathered courage to ask him the reason for his agitation. The sultan was gracious enough and replied in these words: 'Listen, God has made me the master of my people and I am expected to be of help to them. This has set me thinking that if I spend all that I have in the treasury—say 100 times more than at present—even that would not suffice to benefit the entire population, not even if I distribute all my wealth to the villages. Out of this worry, a solution came to my mind and I'll tell you what it was. I hit upon the idea of devising a method to reduce the prices of foodgrains. The way out was to issue a farman to nodal chiefs as well as to those who bring their goods to the city. Some of them bring large swathes of cloth ranging from one to twenty thousand rolls. I would give clothes, allowances for household expenses, and pay them in silver if they brought their goods directly here. It would attract them to bring their grains here and they would sell them at the price fixed by me.' Consequently, he issued the royal order. After this order, foodgrains started arriving from all directions and the cheap rates ultimately benefited the people.

The sultans of Delhi issued coins and currency of their own as is the hallmark of every ruler of note. The most well-known was the coin of Qutbuddin Aibak's times, known as *dehliwal*. An inscription on the Qutub Minar mentions the expense for the construction of a mosque as 5 crore and 50 lakh dehliwal. The coin was still in currency during Balban's time, when it had an ox with a rider etched on one side. Later, the jetal came to replace the dehliwal. Gold coins were also minted for some time as had been the case during the Rajput period. Interestingly, the coins of Shahabuddin bore the image of Lakshmi. Altamash issued the silver tanka, with about 96 *rati* (a measure of weight equal to eight barley corns) silver in it, and both jetal and tanka were in circulation, with some change, under Mohammad bin Tughlaq. The coin of the lowest denomination was *yagani*, then came *sultani, shashgani, hashtgani, dawazdagani*, and *shanzdagani*. After these coins of low denominations, came the tanka, equal to four shanzdagani. A gold coin equalled 10 silver tankas.

There happened to be a global shortage of silver in the time of Mohammad bin Tughlaq, and he found a solution by introducing a 'token coin' (*mohurma*) in place of the silver coins. However, it was a disastrous scheme because it wasn't backed by strict and watchful implementation. It led to the circulation of counterfeit coins. Every house turned into a mint. The people went about freely buying weapons, horses, et cetera, with such coins, not even hesitating to use them for paying taxes and state dues. They were then ordered to deposit them in the state treasury, and there were virtually mountain heaps of bad coins deposited. The sultan reverted to the old system, converting both silver and gold coins into shashgani and *dogani* coins.

DELHI'S *SERAIS*

There are various references to the serais of Delhi in the writings and memoirs of the saints, but regrettably without much detail. There are mentions of Arab Serai, Namak ki Serai, Mian Bazaar ki Serai, and Serai Rakabdar. It seems these serais came up at different stages serving different purposes. In Delhi and Ferozabad, 120 khaneqahs built by Feroz Shah were in fact serais. In the words of Afif, the serais were built to accommodate travellers.

بدیں نیت کہ چوں مسافراں از اطراف و اکناف جہاں دریں مکاں بیایند،
در ہر خانقا کسان سہ روز مہمان باشند۔

*The aim was that the travellers coming from around the world
could stay as guests in the khaneqah for three days.*

They provided all the conveniences but were affordable for people with low income as well.

When Shaikh Nizamuddin Aulia moved to Delhi from Badayun with his mother and sister, he first stayed at Namak Serai.[72] Later, he moved to a small room in the crowded Serai Rakabdar. He eventually found a permanent abode where his family could live comfortably. References to serais in the writings and sayings of the saints provide interesting glimpses into

[72] Kirmani, *Sair-ul Aulia*, p. 115.

the living conditions at inns of those days. During winter, travellers who came to these serais were served khichri. The wealthy used to build serais near palaces, leaving them in the care of influential people of the locality. The caretakers tried their best to keep the atmosphere intact. Overall, the ambience of the inns was pleasant.

DELHI'S GARDENS

Arab travellers visiting Delhi in the 14th century spoke of miles and miles of sprawling gardens and fruit orchards in the north and south-east of Delhi.[73] These were picnic spots for recreation and for holding feasts and musical concerts. The Bagh-e-Jasrat was located near Hauz Rani.[74] Sufis also chose lonely spots in these gardens for meditation. Sultan Feroz Tughlaq was especially fond of gardens and, according to Afif, he had as many as 1,200 gardens developed in and around Delhi. These gardens combined flowerbeds of myriad hues with orchards of grapes, apples, lemons, pomegranates, oranges, and figs.[75] Grapes of as many as seven varieties could be found in Delhi and were produced in such an abundance that they were sold at the rate of one jetal per seer.

[73] Qalqashandī, *Subh-ul Asha*, p. 29.

[74] Kirmani, *Sair-ul Aulia*, p. 118.

[75] Burni, *Tareekh-e Firoz*, pp. 569–70.

They fetched an annual income of one lakh and eighty thousand tankas for the sultan. Musk melon was sold at a jetal a maund during Balban's time. It became cheaper still in Feroz Shah's time.

The network of canals built by Feroz Shah Tughlaq contributed greatly to the thriving of gardens and orchards. Varieties of fruit earlier brought from abroad started to be cultivated in Delhi.

DELHI'S HOSPITALS

In the 14th century, Delhi had as many as 70 hospitals called *darul shifa*, dispensing free medical aid. Feroz Shah founded a large hospital named Sehat Khana. It had physicians of great repute and employed surgeons and pharmacists in large numbers. Patients were dispensed medicines and meals free of cost in the hospitals of Delhi. According to Afif, so accomplished were the physicians employed in these hospitals that even those patients who were afflicted with serious problems and had to rest at every step would go back home fully recuperated, walking briskly.

DELHI'S GRAVEYARDS

According to famous traveller Ibn-e-Batuta, the cemeteries of Delhi were located outside the Bajalasa

Darwaza in an atmosphere of calm and serenity. The graves of even common people were topped with domes and had uniform niches and flowerbeds. Those of the affluent were far grander, of course, much more so in the case of the rulers.

Ibn-e-Batuta himself held charge of the tomb of Mubarak Khilji. He employed 150 reciters of the Holy Quran called *khatmi*. There was provision for the meals of 80 students. The employees included an imam, muezzin, teachers, water carriers, paan sellers, orderlies, and ushers, known collectively as *hashia*. The entire staff numbered 450, for whom 35 maunds of meat was cooked every day. Ibn-e-Batuta documents interesting burial practices:

People in Hindustan place articles of everyday use along with trinkets in the graves. They also tie up elephants and horses near the graves. They decorate the graves.[76]

Only two royal tombs in Delhi, one of Razia Sultan and the other of Alauddin Khilji, were venerated by the people. The visitors tied votive threads with prayers to the grill at the grave of Alauddin Khilji, praying for their wishes to be granted.

Finally, the picture of society that emerges from contemporary accounts is one of cultural synthesis of

[76] Husain, *Ajaib-ul Asfar*, pp. 225–6.

traditions born in the khaneqah and the durbar, and no less in the bazaar. Together they brought down the narrow dividing walls of language and rigid social mores without which a cultural confluence could not have taken root and flourished.

This concept of synthesis drew strength from the Sufi thought best illustrated in the mode of conduct of disciples at the khaneqah of Hazrat Nizamuddin Aulia. His disciples were all brothers, irrespective of faith and belief. Whenever a Muslim visitor came with a Hindu friend, he introduced him in these words, 'This is my brother.' This sentence encapsulates the wonderfully inclusive social fabric of Delhi. Once, someone referred to Hindus as kafirs in the presence of Shaikh Hamiduddin Nagori, only to earn a sharp rebuke from the saint, who said: 'Do you know about the man and his spiritual depth?' His approach earned him the applause of Shaikh Nizamuddin Aulia. In sum, love and reverence for human beings was the basis of the cultural ethos of Delhi in those days.

A sense of communal harmony and tolerance prevailed. Hindu processions passing close by the royal fort playing music were a common sight. Burni recalls how much the scene of Hindu pilgrims—men and women—passing by the fort pleased Jalaluddin Khilji. He quoted Alauddin Khilji, 'Hindus pass every day by the royal palace while singing and playing music.'

Indeed, people in the thousands would take their bath and worship idols in the morning on the banks of the Jamuna. A stone inscription in Purana Qila refers in Persian and Sanskrit to the grant of 12 bighas of land to Shri Krishna mandir. Hindu festivals were a picture of 'music, singing, and gaiety'. Holi celebrations were a regular feature in the durbar of Mohammed bin Tughlaq and the sultan held prolonged counsel with jogis and Jain *munis* (holy men). Khusrau, in his work *Nau Sipihr*, is full of praise for the work of scholars in the pre-Muslim era, regarding himself as part of this heritage. The composite social life of Delhi boosted people's morale to the extent that they firmly believed that they were an integral part of the cultural life of India, irrespective of their religion and creed. It brought people on to one platform, creating a bond of kinship. As a result, a Brahmin could become a teacher at a centre of Islamic education during the medieval period. To the utter astonishment of Badayuni:

باوجود کفر کتب علم رسمی را درس می گفت

Despite being an unbeliever, he taught from traditional books of high learning.

The invasion and plunder by Timur disrupted and destroyed this fabric of harmony, even though the process of political decline of the sultanate had already begun soon after the death of Feroz Shah, ultimately limiting the sultan's control from Delhi to Palam. Timur destroyed the tottering structure, putting an end to the continuity of successive governance. In his memoirs, he ascribed this to the 'will of God', thereby absolving himself of the responsibility of the destruction of Jahan Panah, Siri, and the old city. Besides, he blamed a section of the local people for going on the offensive against his army. However it may be, the ulema and poets left Delhi in the wake of his invasion and settled in other parts of the country. Timur took away many craftsmen to Samarkand, their departure creating a vacuum which took about 150 years to fill—only when the descendents of Timur came to rule over the country was Delhi restored to its former glory.

2

Delhi under the Mughals

....

After Timur's invasion, the centre of political
and cultural activity shifted from Delhi to the
provinces, and the civilizational achievements that had
so far been limited to Delhi were extended to the smaller
metropolises of Pandwa, Lakhnauti, Daulatabad,
Burhanpur, Zainabad, Mandu, and Ahmedabad. At the
time autonomous governments were already in power
in Bengal, Gujarat, Malwa, and the Deccan, which
shaped their own cultural fabrics.

By the beginning of the 16th century, when Babar
turned his attention towards India, these provincial
governments had declined and become weak. The
political system of the Afghans had also declined. There
was chaos and anarchy and a process of renewal was
urgently required to rescue the culture and civilization
of the country. Akbar tried to amalgamate the different
strands of culture, making use of the rich provincial
traditions. The Mahabharata was translated in Bengal
at the insistence of Nusrat Shah. This was followed by

translations of works such as Saghir's *Yusuf-Zulekha*, Behram's *Laila Majnu*, and Afzal Ali's *Nasihatnama*, which successfully integrated the traditions of Iran and Hindustan. Chaitanya, a Bhakti saint of note in Bengal, along with others elsewhere, paved the way for religious progressiveness. Husain Shah founded the Sita Peer tradition which was, again, a movement to cement the bonds between Hindus and Muslims.

Jaunpur, nicknamed the second Delhi,[1] evolved as a centre of this growing tradition of religious tolerance. Its buildings were standing symbols of Hindu and Muslim architectural harmony. Similar developments were taking place in Gujarat, Malwa, and the Deccan. This process of evolution in the provinces became an asset for Mughal rulers and for the Delhi of Mughal times. Amid reconstruction, old traditions that had survived the ravages of time were revived. It was like the proverbial return of the prodigal son to fulfil a new role. Perhaps it was just another instance of the cyclical nature of civilizations. In any case, a cultural study of old Delhi families that had left amid adversity but returned in the Mughal period would indeed prove meaningful and rewarding for our current discussion.

[1] Abul Qasim Farishta, *Tareekh-e Farishta*, vol. II, Bombay, 1832, p. 306.

DELHI'S EVOLUTION UNDER THE MUGHALS

Delhi was not restored to its pivotal position as the political and cultural centre even after the establishment of Mughal rule in India. The balance tilted in favour of Agra because its strategic location made it easier to control the Rajputana region. As a result Delhi did not regain its lost glory till Emperor Shahjehan moved the capital from Agra back to Delhi.

In 1533, Humayun laid the foundation of the city of Dinpanah on the banks of the Jamuna in Delhi. Within a period of 10 months, the gates and walls of the city were constructed, using material from the ruins of Alauddin Khilji's Siri. However, Sher Shah Suri, on his ascendency to power, systematically destroyed every structure raised by Humayun, leaving no trace of Dinpanah. Instead, Sher Shah built a new city alongside the river, near Inderpat, in 1541. This was adjacent to Kotla Feroz Shah. The mosque at Purana Qila and Sher Mandal also came up during his reign. On his return to power, Humayun built a library at Sher Mandal which Sher Shah had used as a spot for leisure activities.

Humayun had deep interest in the study of the universe—in both astronomy and astrology. This was reflected in the hierarchy of his durbar, which he divided into three strata. The first comprised people of wealth and rank such as viziers, the army brass, emirs, and his close relatives; in the next rank were placed the ulema and shaikhs along with poets; the third included men of the arts, music, and entertainment. Interestingly, Humayun gave them planetary identities and colours. His durbaris wore apparel in colours corresponding to the supposed colours of the particular heavenly body associated with their group. Humayun even fixed his meetings with courtiers according to their planetary days; for instance Tuesday, related to the planet Mars, was earmarked for meetings with the army brass. The tents in the durbar were erected according to astronomical principles. The seating arrangement was also designed according to stellar positions: the first, the entertainment section, was arranged in line with *falak-e atlas* or the Milky Way; the second was sky blue; and the third was black, the colour associated with Saturn.

Humayun's obsession with astronomy and astrology filtered down to the common people as well. Sufis such as Syed Mohammad Ghaus of Gwalior and his brother Shaikh Behlul, who believed in the power of stars and their influence on human lives under divine intervention, moved to Delhi as they were much sought after for their predictions.

An interesting construction in Humayun's time was a floating palace (Mahal-e-Rawan) on the river Jamuna. It was constructed by tying together four boats. These had separate niches and an artificial pool was located between them. Yet, their arrangement was such that while moving on the waterway they looked like a single unit. The king and his consorts as well as noblemen closest to the king travelled on this floating palace from Delhi to Agra. Many other boats carrying articles for sale followed in tow, from which people purchased commodities of need. Some boats even had gardens, while others carried song-and-dance parties and their performances 'enthralled even Venus into dancing'.[2]

However, neither Humayun nor Sher Shah could return Delhi to its former glory; the credit for that belongs almost in entirety to Shahjehan. Following Shahjehan, the cultural synthesis of Hindustan revolved around Delhi for the next 200 or so years. So it is not very surprising that the Hindus and Muslims gathered as one entity against the machinations of the English in 1857, with Bahadur Shah Zafar as the figurehead. Bahadur Shah became the symbol and focal point of Indian resistance, despite his obvious limitations evident from the fact that he was likened to a setting sun. As a result, the Marathas who were involved in a political confrontation with the Mughals too joined in and the Peshwa unhesitatingly accepted the leadership of Bahadur Shah at this critical juncture of history.

[2] Khawand Meer, *Qanoon-e-Humayuni*, ed. M. Hidayat Husain, Calcutta, 1940.

SHAHJEHANABAD

In 1638, the 12th year of his reign, Shahjehan finally embarked on the foundation of the new capital—Shahjehanabad—marking the rebirth of Delhi. It started with the construction of the imposing Lal Qila (Red Fort), which took about 10 years to complete. Shahjehan himself moved into the fort in 1648. The old waterway of Nahr-i-Shahab was cleaned up, while another lengthy canal was constructed, running through the middle of Chandni Chowk and adding to the razzle dazzle of the city's main shopping thoroughfare. Altamash had already bestowed a distinct identity upon Delhi through the Qutub Minar and Hauz-e-Shamsi; Shahjehan built the Lal Qila and Jama Masjid as the hubs and axes of the city. The capital reached the peak of its glory with the newly constructed water tanks and reservoirs, and canals adorned with sprouting fountains. The Diwan-e-Aam, Diwan-e-Khas, Takht-e-Taus (the Peacock Throne), and the *hamam*s (bathing chambers) along with their appurtenances displayed the emperor's highly developed aesthetic sensibilities and were symbols of his artistic and refined taste. The fort was both magnificent and charming. Its outer gate was named Lahori Darwaza and provided unhindered access to Chandni Chowk; two life-sized stone elephants flanked the southern gate named Delhi Darwaza, symbolizing the majesty of the empire.

Shahjehan, a patron of art and culture, also realized the value of recreation and merrymaking in the lives of his subjects. This was the purpose of the Meena Bazaar. He loved watching elephant fights as much as he admired the poetics of Qudsi, Abu Talib Kaleem, Shadna, and Saeeda-e-Geelani. He was equally appreciative of the work of Sanskrit and Hindi poets—Sunder, Shambhunath, and Chintamani—who flourished under his patronage.

Inside the fort was a world in itself, with the durbar as the axis; François Bernier has provided interesting insight into the activities of the fort. The road from Delhi Darwaza that led into the fort had a canal along its middle. There were raised platforms 6 feet tall and 4 feet wide, on both sides of the road, followed by long arched verandas opening into vast spaces, accommodating those who were in charge of workshops, lower rank officials, and watchmen. The *mansabdar*s (delegated officials) deputed for night duty would also use the platforms for resting. The canal water ran from the royal quarters to other houses before draining out into the moat around the fort. The canal was connected to the Jamuna, some 15 or 18 miles from the fort.

A long road from Lahori Darwaza, with platforms on both sides, also led into the fort. It was flanked by a row of shops. It also branched into walkways leading to yet another row of houses used by noblemen on special duty during the night. These houses had expensive furnishings, the emirs bearing the cost of these embellishments. The houses were built on the pattern of the Diwan-e-Khas, with graceful gardens in front complete with gushing fountains and variegated flower beds. Food for the officers on special duty would come from the palace and it was a sight to see the elite bowing low towards the palace in humility and gratitude for their meals. Many other offices were also located inside the fort, and craftsmen, artisans, sculptors, as well as those engaged in polishing work had their workplaces within the complex. Others such as carpenters, shoemakers, tailors, and those engaged in chikan, filigree, and silk and velvet artwork and painting too worked nearby.

Tailoring was a great art in those days. Some tailors used cloth of such a fine weave that it required highly delicate and fine needlework to stitch it and was fit for only a single night's use. These artisans would turn up for duty early in the morning and work through the day.

The walkway led to a huge square house surrounded by arches. On its roof sat pipers and *shehnai* (a wind instrument) players. This was the Naqqarkhana from where drums were beaten at specified times. The pleasant sound of drum beats travelled a long distance. Nearby, in front of the picture gallery, there was a large enclosure with golden pillars and ceiling. It was built on a high pedestal and was open on three sides. The emperor sat in the Nasheman Zille-Ilahi (resting place for the shadow of God) in the daytime. Princes stood on the left and right of the emperor and eunuchs with plumed staffs kept the flies away. Under the king's pedestal, there was an enclosure with silver railings, in which stood the rajas, noblemen, and envoys. The rest of the enclosure accommodated commoners. That is why this court was for both commoners and the elite. According to the records of Khani Khan, no other monarch had constructed such a large Darbar-e-Aam, with special provision to shelter the people from the harsh sun and heavy rains. The routine of salutations over, it would be time for supplicants among the common people to present their complaints before the emperor. In the meantime, horses were brought, followed by tame elephants decorated with red lines running from their heads to the trunks, their backs bedecked with brocade sheets and two silver bells hanging from silver chains—the bells also had tails of Tibetan cows, giving the impression of long moustaches. They saluted the emperor with raised trunks. After the elephants came tame antelolpes, nilgai, deer, rhinos, and buffaloes from Bengal, and hounds from Bukhara. Last came the turn of predatory birds of various species.

After the show, the business of government began with petitions presented to the emperor. Shahjehan made it a point to personally attend to the grievances of the citizenry at private sittings. In these strictly private sittings, he also attended to the grievances of 10 poor people chosen from the group of complainants. When a good word issued from the emperor's lips, everyone looked towards the sky and uttered, 'It is a miracle.' He also went through the submissions of the emirs and officials of state while disposing of other official matters.

Between the Diwan-e-Khas and Diwan-e-Aam was a private apartment known as *ghusl khana,* where the emperor listened to the submissions of the nobility and subedars and all important matters of state were discussed. A strict code of conduct was prescribed for meetings and those not turning up regularly in the morning had to pay fines; those emirs who absented themselves in the evening were liable to other forms of punishment. The reason for this strict insistence on attendance on the part of Shahjehan was that he himself was highly punctilious about attending to the affairs of the state, missing the routine only if he was very ill. The mansabdars on duty paid him respectful obeisance and proceeded to attend to their duties.

Shahjehan was a very God-fearing man. An early riser, he would go to the mosque near his personal quarters for morning prayers and spend quality performing prayers and rituals. Sunrise was darshan time at the *jharoka* (lattice). Later, he enjoyed watching elephant fights and routinely inspected the army contingent. He would then move on to the Diwan-e-Aam, spending a few hours there, and would then proceed to the Diwan-e-Khas. The next halt was Shahburj where he would spend time with the princes and a select few.

After the *asr* (second prayer of the day in the early afternoon) he would go to the palace and have his lunch. Shahjehan was very fond of food and took personal interest in the preparation of a variety of foods. New cuisines introduced during his time were documented in a rare booklet called *Dastoor-e Pukhtan-e Ta'am*, now stored in the library of Aligarh Muslim University. After lunch, he took a siesta. There were only begums and princes in attendance at this time. After *zuhr* (third prayer of the day in the late afternoon), he would again sit at the jharoka before *namaz-e-maghrib* (fourth prayer of the day) at the Diwan-e-Khas. He still had time to listen to songs and music till *isha* (night prayers), after which he would go to Shahburj to check up on the day's remaining work before retiring to bed. Soft notes of music and songs of maidens and readers reading out to him some passages from books from behind a curtain would finally lull him to sleep.

Meena Bazaar

The Meena Bazaar, in fact, began in the time of Emperor Akbar, as Abul Fazal records. But it reached the peak of its

elegance only during the rule of Shahjehan. Bernier has
given interesting details about a make-believe bazaar, the
shops set up by the spouses of emirs and mansabdars
selling expensive velvets and brocaded finery. The
emperor and his begums and daughters, along with the
wives of the nobles, acted as customers. The fun lay in
the spectacle of the emperor and his begums engaged
in haggling over prices, the exchange between customer
and shopkeeper marked by heated argument, banter,
and colloquialisms of the marketplace. The emperor
would say that such and such begum was selling at
rather high prices and add that he would not waste even
a penny on her wares. He would advocate going to some
other shop. The shopkeepers would reply that as the
emperor did not know the value of the articles sold there,
he had better go to some cheaper shops. The begums of
the emperor wanted to buy things cheap. On occasion
there would even be mock fights, but once the deal was
reached and bargain made, silver and gold coins would
rain down. It seemed as if the emperor, his begums, and
his daughters were bewitched by the shopkeepers and
their daughters and they would be paid lavishly.

Moonlit Night Carnival

Shahjehan was fond of holding celebratory gatherings
and, expectedly, the occasions were marked by beauty

and grace. Often, he thought of some new ideas which added to the elegance of the celebration. Once he thought of holding a function on a moonlit night. It was held in front of the Diwan-e-Aam, with the furnishings matching the silvery moonlight—white velvet carpets and white brocade curtains for the walls, white lamps of ivory, white flowers, white shades on carefully handpicked plants, white grass strewn on the pathways. The attendees also wore pristine clothes, with silver rings on their fingers.

ALAMGIR'S CORONATION

Delhi was witness to the rise and fall of many a ruler and king and their coronation ceremonies. But in terms of resplendence, the coronation of Aurangzeb Alamgir by far exceeded them all in pomp and show, and indeed in riches. Delhi had already become a treasure trove of vast wealth in the time of Shahjehan. His son Alamgir had all of this at his disposal, including the Lal Qila and the Takht-e Taus that Shahjehan did not have at the time of his coronation.

Alamgir entered Delhi after bitter fighting and felling his rivals and he needed something to stamp his authority as emperor. The victory procession entered Delhi amid unprecedented fanfare, with drummers, pipers, and flautists leading the way. They were followed by an unending row of elephants caparisoned in velvet and brocade, with the royal flag flying atop each, their howdahs embroidered with pearls, silver chains jingling around their legs, and their trunks brightly painted. Behind them came horses with gilded saddlery and pearl-studded bridles, and troops marching with bare swords in hand, led by noblemen walking just ahead. Finally, the emperor came riding on elephant back with armed guards maintaining sharp vigil. There was a heavy shower of gold and silver coins all along the way.

The procession reached Lahori Darwaza, the main entrance to the fort, and all alighted. The final stop was the Diwan-e-Aam, which was lavishly decorated for the big event. There was an array of light and colour, the pillars and ceilings bedecked in gold, velvet, and expensive varieties of silk from Iran and Gujarat. Lit lamps hung on the arches from golden chains. There was of course the Takht-e-Taus in all its opulence, with emerald, diamonds, and pearls adding to its effulgence. The peacock feathers carved in the throne were studded with expensive gems. A canopy supported by 12 pillars and laden with dazzling jewels was erected over the throne. Royal paintings bedecked the walls. Nothing but gems and jewels met the eye, from floor to ceiling. The royal retinue turned up in its best livery as if to accentuate the resplendence of the event. The pomp and show were indeed without parallel in Delhi's long history.

LITERARY TASTE OF THE MUGHAL EMPERORS

The Mughals were known for their impeccable literary taste and while they had scholars and poets of exceptional brilliance in the court, many of them were themselves writers and poets of excellence. Along with an interest in astronomy and astrology, Humayun wrote excellent verses in Persian. His work displayed subtle flights of imagination as well as a powerful style of expression. Aurangzeb's interests were limited to matters of faith and religion. The pages of *Fatawa-e-Alamgiri*, a religious compendium, were presented to him for suitable corrections. Later Mughal royals, Mohammed Shah, Farrukh Siyar, Shah Alam, and Bahadur Shah Zafar, all had a flair for poetry. The begums and other royal women also did not lag behind. Shahjehan's daughter Jahanara and Aurangzeb's daughter Zebunnisa were renowned for their love of the arts. Zebunnisa even founded the Bait-ul-Hikmat (house of wisdom) for which the ulema wrote books, dedicating them to the princess. The titles of the books were all prefixed with 'Zeb', *Zeb-usTafsir* being one of them.

NOBLES

The nobles of the court were fond of building imposing mansions replicating the Lal Qila, based on their

individual capacity and means. Thus there was a mini
Lal Qila for every emir. Till the time of Alamgir, the
Mughal nobility was on the whole learned, cultured,
and dedicated to working for the welfare of the people.
If they indulged in merrymaking occasionally, it was
for relaxation and to take a break from the rigours of a
hectic life of war and politics. Overall, they were devoted
to art and literature combined with an overwhelming
desire to be of service to the people. Some of them
had engaged men of learning of European origin to
keep themselves abreast of the advances in the West
in various disciplines. Shaikh Farid Nawab Murtaza
Khan attained wide acclaim during this time. Born in
Delhi during the Akbar–Jehangir era, he grew up to be
a great philanthropist. Akbar gifted him the beautiful
Saleemgarh situated near the fort. The Jamuna flowed
close by, lending the landscape particular charm and
character. During the famine of 1595–8, he came to
the rescue of the poor and was reputed to have spent
more than he could afford for the purpose. It is said
that whenever he ventured out of the house he made
it a point to take all kinds of clothing, including gowns,
quilts, and blankets to distribute among the needy. He
also gave them money, making regular payments to
widows and destitutes. He looked after the education of
the children of employees who died in his service. In
Faridabad, a town near Delhi, many houses and tanks

stand as reminders of his generosity. People say the nawab never built a house for himself and led the life of an ever-travelling passenger, considering the world a transitory place. He fed one thousand people every day, half of them getting the food in their homes, while the rest dined with him in his home.

Overall, the nobles with their high ethical standards and love of learning and culture were a positive force in society. For example, there was Danishmand Khan, who was known for his extensive library. The emperor, in view of Danishmand Khan's thirst for knowledge and love of books, had exempted him from daily attendance at the court. Danishmand Khan studied Western science to understand the progress made by the West. He got many French books translated, and even conducted experiments to understand various scientific discoveries.

However, after the end of Aurangzeb's rule, the rich and wealthy became a debauched lot, interested only in wine and song and dance. Jahandar Shah spent lakhs of rupees on the courtesan Lal Kanwar. He is said to have wasted huge sums of money on lighting for his recreational sessions and revelries, leading to shortage of oil in Delhi and sending oil prices skyrocketing. As recorded in *Muraqqa-e Dehli*, Wazir-ul Mulk Etmadud Daula gifted a wine jar and glass to a courtesan that cost 70,000 rupees! Both Hindu and Muslim nobles were equally careless spendthrifts. Raja Jugal Kishore extended a general public invitation to the inhabitants of Delhi on the occasion of the wedding of his son Anand Kishore. When those of the upper class felt hesitant to accept a general invitation, the raja personally called on them, begging them to come to the wedding to 'bless their nephew'. The raja had frittered away his entire fortune. It is said that when the great poet Mir Taqi Mir went to him for a grant, the raja said that he had nothing to offer except his tattered shawl: 'I would not have hesitated to offer something more expensive if I had been in a position to do so.'[3] This was in no way an exception; hundreds of emirs and people of wealth were facing the same dilemma after having squandered all their wealth.

LANES AND BAZAARS

The construction of the majestic palaces and forts of the rulers and nobility provided a major source of employment to the poor. Many of the nobility had built mansions in Delhi to stay in comfort during their visits to the city, accompanied by a retinue of guards and other staff. It is difficult to imagine the beauty and vastness of these houses which often shone like jewels amidst

---

[3] Maulvi Abdul Haq, *Zikr-e Mir*, Anjuman-e Urdu Press, Hyderabad, 1928, p. 78.

the general darkness. This inspired Mirza Ghalib's famous couplet when he went to meet his friend Nawab Mustafa Khan Shaifta: 'The stream of elixir is situated in extreme darkness,' said Ghalib. On reaching the *diwan khana* (hall of audience) and seeing the sun-soaked veranda, he further recited: 'This entire abode dazzles as the sun.'[4]

Most of the houses located in the lanes of Delhi were built along the same pattern. The mohallas, bazaars, chowks, *katra*s (market, or a part of city), *kucha*s (narrow streets), havelis, and *chhatta*s (covered streets) were often named after some nobleman or the other. Sangeen Beg wrote in his *Sair-ul-Manaazil* that most of the craftsmen had set up their shops in specific areas even before 1857. For instance, Hauz Qazi had shops of carpenters and those making goods out of reed. In Kucha Pandit were the bangle shops and in Kucha Saadullah were bird catchers and butchers. Dariba Kalan had goldsmiths, silversmiths, and jewellers. There were other localities where cloth merchants, washermen, vegetable sellers, or those engaged in ornamentation or engravings were concentrated. These localities had names such as Rudgaran, Churigaran, Khatikon ka Kucha, Kucha Batashe Wala, Sabzi Mandi, Paan Dariba,

[4] Khwaja Altaf Husain Hali, *Yadgar-e Ghalib*, Maktaba Jamia, Delhi, 1981.

Jauhari Bazaar, and Dhobiwada. A study of a few of these mohallas would bring many interesting aspects of Delhi's social history to light.

A bazaar existed at virtually every street corner but there were seven major shopping centres in the city, one of them running right up to the main gate of the fort, another at the very threshold of the Lahori Darwaza. Here there were two-storey shops with arches and storehouses behind. The shop owners slept in the upper storey at night. Those rooms that opened out on the bazaar were particularly attractive. Most of the shopkeepers owned godowns for safely housing their goods. Tourists were critical of Shahjehan's Delhi on two counts: swarms of flies at *halwai* (confectioner) shops and the inferior quality and dubious type of meat served at eating houses. The French physician François Bernier, who was the personal physician to Dara Shikoh, Shahjehan's eldest son, and was subsequently attached to Aurangzeb's court, wrote to a friend in Paris that at times camel or horse meat, even that of a dead ox, passed off as mutton.[5]

Fortune tellers, astrologers, and astronomers abounded in the bazaars, invariably seated on tattered carpets and armed with worn-out gadgets and books

---

[5] François Bernier, *Travels in the Mughal Empire*, Paris, 1670, p. 250.

with zodiac signs. Women wrapped in white sheets were seen surrounding them in large numbers. The markets were filled with clothes. Fine fabrics made in Delhi as well as those imported from other countries were available in Delhi. The fruit market was located away from the main hub and all varieties of fruit from Iran, Balkh, Bukhara, and Samarkand were sold there. Grapes and pears of three or four kinds wrapped in cotton were available. *Sarda* (a kind of melon) was the costliest fruit. One sarda cost about 4 rupees. Though expensive, it was a favourite of the people of Delhi, as also of the nobles. Dry fruit too was available in abundance. It is said that 20 gold coins worth of dry fruit was served at the breakfast table of Danishmand Khan every day. Birds were available in the market aplenty.

Purchasing liquor was not easy. Wines of Shiraz were very costly and not many could afford them. Indian liquor, called *araq*, on the other hand, was very strong and there were restrictions on its sale.

There was a surfeit of goods in the market. However, the prices of luxury and imported goods were very high. There is the story of the scion of an affluent family asking his mother for money for shopping. The mother gave him a sum of 1 lakh rupees, regretting that she could not afford to give more for rare items.

Delhi in those days had a string of *qahwa khana*s (tea/ coffee houses) which served as meeting places for poets and men of letters. Dargah Quli Khan has written about the tea houses that were situated right in the heart of Chandni Chowk and patronized on a daily basis by poets and writers who received great adulation. Chowk Saadullah was next to Chandni Chowk in importance. Apart from the atmosphere of merriment, dance, and creativity, it was also a hub for preachers extolling the virtues of fasting and Hajj. According to Dargah Quli Khan these tea houses yielded good money for people, with fortune tellers, astrologers, and quacks selling medicines using them for their businesses.

JAMA MASJID

The foundations of the Jama Masjid were laid by Shahjehan in the 24th year of his reign on 10 Shawwal, 1060 Hejra (18 October 1649) and it was completed over a period of 6 years at a cost of about 10 lakh rupees. Some five thousand masons, stone cutters, and labourers worked on the construction every day. In charge of the proceedings was famed architect and builder Ahmad who also supervised the construction of the Red Fort and the Taj Mahal. He excelled in geography, astronomy, and mathematics and had earned the confidence of the emperor. Ahmad was known for his deep knowledge of the works of famous Persian polymath architect Khawaja Naseer Tusi. Shahjehan conferred the title of Nidir-e-Asr

on Ahmad. Lutfullah Mohandis writes about him in a
mathnawi/masnawi (a poem in which the second line of
each distich rhymes with the same letter):

احمد معمار کہ درفن خویش

صد قدم از اہل ہنر بود بیش

واقف تحریر و مقامات آں

آگہ اشکال و حوالات آں

از طرف داور گردوں جناب

نادر عصر آمدہ اور اخطاب

Architect Ahmad was miles ahead of other craftsmen.
He was well versed in Tahreer, a book,
and fully understood the graphs and maps:
he was conferred the title of Nadir-e-Asr
by Shahjehan (the commander of the skies).

Shahjehan had the layout of the mausoleum of
Mumtaz Mahal, the Taj Mahal, prepared by Ahmad.
Another mathnawi couplet marks his role in the
building of the Taj Mahal:

کرد بحکم شہ کشور کشا

روضہ ممتاز محل رابنا

At the bidding of the Lord of the Land
He erected the mausoleum of Mumtaz Mahal.

Ahmad had three sons, Attaullah, Lutfullah, and Nurullah; all of them were master architects and builders in their own right.

مابمہ معمار و عمارت گریم

مابمہ استاد و سخن پروریم

We are all builders and architects,
and are masters in our crafts and also appreciate the art of poetry.

An inscription on the gates of the Jama Masjid in Delhi is testimony to Nurullah's refined handiwork. The inscription bears his name. The great savant and religious philosopher Shah Kaleemullah of Delhi was the son of Nurullah. Azad Bilgrami has written about him that while his forbears were masons engaged in constructing buildings made of cement and bricks and mortar, Shah Kaleemullah was engaged in cementing hearts.

The Jama Masjid was indeed the heart of Shahjehanabad's social life. Built atop a hill, it was surrounded by a rectangular open space. Four markets from the four sides joined each other at the doorstep of this grand mosque, as noted by Bernier.[6] At the southern gate, huge crowds gathered in the afternoon, including peddlers of ice *faluda* (a vermicelli-like dish), kebabs,

---

[6] Bernier, *Travels in the Mughal Empire*, p. 301.

and cooked chicken. Mohsin Dehlvi portrays the scene in the following couplet:

سناتے پھرتے تھے سقّے کٹوروں کی جھنکار

وہ گل فروشوں کے پھولوں کے ٹوکروں کی بہار

وہ سودا بیچتے تھے لوگ واں پُکار پُکار

وہ پھرنا خوانچے والوں کا واں قطار قطار

رکھا تھا دہلی کا لوگوں نے نام عشق آباد

بسانِ خانۂ عاشق وہ ہوگئی برباد

Water carriers went about jingling their bowls,
Just as flower sellers had flowers aplenty in bloom,
Vendors shouted out their wares in loud voices,
Peddlers flaunting baskets with cooked peas moved in rows,
People had aptly named Delhi 'Ishqabad'
But it lay in ruins as the lover's abode.

There were vendors and kebab shops at the northern gate also, but the place was better known as a hub for magicians, jugglers and charmers, and narrators of fables sitting on leather stools as they retold tales from *Dastan-e-Amir Hamza, Hatim Tai,* and *Bostan-e-Khayal.* People thronged to this gate in hundreds to listen enraptured to these yarns. Plays such as *Bhanmati* were enacted, interpersed with jugglers showing their skills. At the eastern gate, the show of the *guzari* (evening market) was a star fixture. Mohammed Shah beautifully paints a picture of dusk in these busy lanes, calling it the time for guzari in his couplet:

پیری میں نہ کس طرح کروں سیر جہاں کی

دن ڈھلتے ہی بوتا ہے تماشا گذری کا

Oh why should I not trip around the world in my old age,
For as the sun sets, ensues the performance of guzari?

Garment vendors hung their wares from wires as merry young men went round carrying singing birds in cages. One could buy anything in this bazaar, from pigeons to horses. Poets engaged in reciting their verses to small gatherings, preachers giving sermons, and medicine peddlers selling medicines with prescriptions formed the motley crowd at the bazaar.

One day, Sarmad the mystic passed by the bazaar when other poets, including Sarkhush, Nasir Sarhindi, and Bedil, were reciting some verses. The saint gave them a broad smile as he recited:

دیر است کہ افسانہ منصور کہن شد

اکنوں سر نو جلوہ وہم دار و رسن را

The tale of Mansur has now gone old,
I myself would enact a scene of rope and gallows again.

BUILDINGS IN DELHI

The French scholar Bernier arrived in Delhi during
Shahajehan's reign, over 25 years after Shahjehanabad
was established. During his stay, he noticed the absence
of a middle class in the capital. The inhabitants were
either very rich or very poor. The houses were either
magnificent palaces or humble thatched dwellings
inhabited by soldiers or ordinary professionals. The
wealthy had majestic, airy homes surrounded by
charming gardens, with gushing fountains in verandas
and in the middle of the central gates. These homes had
underground vaults with *khas*-grass (sweet-scented root
of a grass), keeping them cool in summer. The vaults
with *khas*-grass were built near the garden and hauz so
that servants could keep them soaked.

In the verandas, thick cotton mattresses were laid.
During summer, the mattresses were covered with
white cotton sheets, and during winter with silk carpets.
For the master of the house and his special guests,
there were mattresses lined with *zari* (gold thread), and
for support there were bolsters of velvet and brocade.
The niches in the veranda were decorated with exotic
Chinese vases and utensils. The ceilings of the central
veranda were often exquisitely painted with murals.[7]

[7] Bernier, *Travels in the Mughal Empire*, p. 248.

The thatched houses made of *khas*-grass and bamboo were also built elegantly. They were properly whitewashed as well.[8] These were not separate structures but part of the main buildings and were prone to catching fire. As many as sixty thousand such thatched houses were gutted by a fire during Aurangzeb's time. Bernier, an eyewitness, recalled that apart from cattle, some women were also burnt alive because they could not run out of the house due to restrictions of purdah.

ARTS AND CRAFTS

In the Mughal era, Delhi was famous for its artisans and craftsmen, both at home and abroad. Many mohallas or neighbourhoods were named after them. Travellers from other countries expressed great admiration for them. Their craftsmanship was of a quality that could compete with that of their European counterparts. Bernier could not but wonder at the delicacy and finery of the cloth used to make the apparel of wives of noblemen. He was equally impressed with the expertise of other artisans such as stone carvers and wood carvers, observing that handmade goods of Indian artisans were as good as the machine-made wares of Europe. He added that it was difficult to distinguish between the handmade and

[8] Bernier, *Travels in the Mughal Empire*, p. 216.

machine-made objects. Again, painting and sculpture were so developed as to be on a par with Europe. Guns made in India were of a quality equal to those of Europe. Gold jewellery of the finest quality was in no way inferior to that crafted in Europe.

Bernier noted that artisans invariably enjoyed the patronage of the royalty and the wealthy. Generally, they did not have workshops of their own, nor did they have any public support as such. This was probably the reason why the artisans also suffered when the royalty and nobility fell on hard times, as Shah Waliullah Dehlavi has mentioned. There is repeated mention of their plight in other chronicles of the times as well.

KHANEQAHS OF DELHI

Only the Chishtia order existed in Delhi during the Sultanate period, but under the Mughals different Sufi orders came to be established and the khaneqahs and seminaries were filled with devotees. The shaikh was the pivot of life in the khaneqah. Many followed the tradition of simple living and fasting. But in certain khaneqahs enjoying the patronage of kings and noblemen, the living conditions were more comfortable. Khwaja Baqi Billah had founded the Naqshbandi order in Delhi. He strengthened the foundations of the order within a remarkably short span of 2 to 3 years. Even though life left him little time to consolidate it, he was able to attract many distinguished personages to his circle by virtue of his sincere conduct. These include disciples such as Shaikh Ahmad Sirhindi, Mujjadadalfsani, and Shaikh Abdul Haq Muhaddis Dehlvi, who were very notable in their respective fields. Shaikh Sirhindi made the Naqshbandi order so popular that its sway spread far and wide and, in the words of Jehangir, his *khalifa*s (Caliphs or successors) could be found in every nook and cranny of the country. Baqi Billah's influence extended to the emirs and included Nawab Murtaza Khan Shaikh Farid, Abdur Rahim Khan Khana, Qaleej Khan, the governor of Punjab, and Mirza Aziz Koka. Khwaja Hisamuddin, brother-in-law of Abul Fazal, had deep faith in him while Nawab Murtaza Khan took the responsibility of bearing the expenses of his khaneqah.

The Naqshbandi order was founded about the same time as the process of renewal began in the Chishtia order. Shaikh Kalimullah Wali occupied a place of special honour and reverence in the order. He rendered yeoman services to the Chishtia order and restored it to its former glory after the death of Hazrat Chirag Dehlvi left it bereft of direction. Gesu Daraz Shaikh, Nur Qutub Alam, Allama Kamaluddin, and others had undisputedly done commendable service in spreading its message; but it lacked a central consolidating force, and that seemed to undermine the very basis of their struggle and spadework. It was thus left to Shah Kalimullah to put the house in order and infuse cohesion. The impact of his efforts to reorder the system and inject into it a spirit of renaissance and renewal was commendable. The shaikh's own khaneqah was located in Bazaar Khanam and was thronged by devotees in search of spiritual solace.

Shaikh Kalimullah lived a life of extreme poverty and hardship but he did not accept offerings even from wealthy emirs or those in power. A haveli for which he received rent of two and a half rupees a month was all he had. He himself lived in another house, making do with merely two rupees to run the household. King Farrukhsiyar offered him money, but the shaikh refused. His disciples were spread all over the country, all the way to the Deccan, but he was able to maintain overall control by meticulously issuing daily instructions even regarding minor issues. The whole town turned up at his *mazaar* (mausoleum) after his death, an index of his immense popularity. However, his mazaar was destroyed in the tragic events of 1857. Ghalib wrote in a letter:

The mausoleum of Shaikh Kalimullah lies in ruins, and the inhabitants are all gone, nor is there any trace of their families. What remains is a jungle and the grave—all else is an empty space. Even if those inhabitants escaped bullet fire, only God knows where they have gone.

The setting up of the khaneqah of Mirza Mazhar Jan-e-Jana was another important development in Delhi's cultural synthesis. He invariably advised those seeking to become his disciples to serve some other shaikh in Delhi as living conditions in his khanequah were very simple and stark. It was only after he had ascertained their sincere interest through their persistence that he accepted them as his disciples and then took great interest in their training. Mirza Mazhar had a broad outlook on religious matters and believed that the Vedas were divine and Hindus too were the 'People of the Book'. He used to explain Hindu rituals and customs to his disciples, thus opening up the way towards mutual understanding. Mirza Saheb endorsed recommendations that he would receive from Hindus without hesitation. He took great interest in Urdu and Persian poetry. Mir Taqi Mir wrote about him in *Nukat-ul-Shura*:

اکثر اوقات دریادالہی صرف می کند، اگرچہ شعر گفتن دون مرتبہ
اوست گاہی متوجہ این بے حاصل می شود۔

He used to spend most of his time remembering the Divine and
even though writing poetry was beneath his dignity, yet at times
he would turn his attention towards the useless art.

The khaneqah of Mirza Saheb's successor, Shah Ghulam Ali, was one of the most illustrious in Delhi, surpassing even Mirza Saheb's. He had one thousand khalifas and disciples in hundreds of thousands. Sir Syed wrote:

I have seen with my own eyes pilgrims from as far places as Rome, Baghdad, Egypt, China and Africa. They visited the *khanqah* to pledge their allegiance to the Shaikh. The visitors from different parts of Hindustan, Punjab and Afgahnistan swarmed the *khaneqah* like locust.

As many as 500 fakirs stayed in his khaneqah and were served meals there. The ruler of Tonk, Amir Mohammed Khan, requested the shaikh to accept his offer of a stipend; the shaikh sent his reply in the form of a couplet:

ما آبروئے فقر و قناعت نمی بریم

با میر خاں بگوے کہ روزی مقرر است

Our hallmark is poverty; self-containment a ritual,
Tell Amir Khan only God can provide one's victuals.

Shahjehanabad had khaneqahs at every step—if there was Chishtia jamaat khana at one spot, there was a Qadriya centre at another; a Rasulshahi lodge here, a Naqshbandi khaneqah elsewhere. According to Shah Abdul Aziz, each family of saints, during the time of Mohammad Shah, had the rare privilege of having 22 holy men in its fold.

MADRASAS

A large number of madrasas existed in Delhi during Mughal times. The rulers, nobles and ulema paid a lot of attention to them. However, they differed widely in terms of both provisioning and the quality of education provided. While those enjoying royal patronage were far better provisioned, this fact did not necessarily make them superior in education. Humayun founded a madrasa which was later shifted to the upper storey of his tomb. It existed there for a long time. It had accommodation for students and a large number of students were enrolled there. In the time of Akbar, Maham Begum built Madrasa Khair-ul-Manazil near Purana Qila. The madrasa built by Shahjehan, which was named Darul Baqa, ran till 1857. There were many other madrasas founded by the Mughal nobles but the madrasas of Shaikh Abdul Haq Mohaddis Dehlvi, Madrasa Rahimia, Madrasa Bazaar Khanam, and the one at Ajmeri Darwaza helped Delhi gain repute in the field of education and turned it into an educational hub, attracting students from far and wide. The madrasa of Mohaddis Dehlavi became the starting point of the movement to promote knowledge of the Hadith.

Famous Egyptian scholar Allama Rashid Ridha conceded that the tradition of teaching and learning Hadith would have come to an end if this branch of learning had not attracted the sincere attention of the Indian ulema in the 10th century. Madrasa Rahimia was a fountainhead of knowledge upon which every other Indian madrasa drew deep. It invigorated religious thinking that wielded influence over the Indian Muslims for a long time. Shah Abd-ur-Rahim and his son, the venerated Shah Waliullah Dehlvi, laid the foundations of a new trend of religious thought. His famed work *Hujjatullah-al-Baligha* was widely appreciated and paved the way for *ilm-e-kalam* (modern scholasticism). His three sons—Shah Abdul Aziz, Shah Abdul Qadir, and Shah Rafiuddin—were all masters of their disciplines. Shah Waliullah translated the Holy Quran into Persian while Shah Abdul Qadir and Shah Rafiuddin translated it into Urdu. These works, along with those by other contemporary scholars, ushered in a virtual revolution in religious thought. Among the works by other scholars was *Lughat-ul Quran* by Shah Abdul Hai, son-in-law of Shah Abdul Aziz. All this helped propagate religious knowledge of a particular school of thought among the masses. Shah Abdul Aziz had acquired mastery over many languages. A contemporary, Maulavi Abdul Qadir Khani, observed that Shah Abdul Aziz had won universal fame for his unique versatility in Hadith, *fiqh* (Islamic jurisprudence), biography, and history as well as mathematics, physics, and logic along with higher understanding of literature and poetry. He saw no harm

in referring to Allah as Parmeshwar. He was also in
favour of learning English and welcomed the advances
in science made in the West. At the same time, he
exhorted the people against foreign domination.

Shah Abdul Aziz was widely respected and had
disciples all over the country. It was generally held
that there was not even a single scholar of the Hadith
anywhere in the country who had not been his pupil.

From his commitment to training young minds
and his enormous influence arose the first sparks of
resistance to foreign rule. Madrasa Rahimia became
one of the first centres of the freedom struggle. Maulana
Syed Ahmed Shaheed and Shah Ismail Shaheed laid
the foundations of their movements in Madrasa Wali-
ul-Lahi. In 1857, when the English embarked on a
mission to destroy all such institutions as were engaged
in spreading the message of freedom, they made all the
centres of the Wali-ul-Lahi school their special target.

Another eminent madrasa was the one established
by Ghaziuddin Khan at the Ajmeri Darwaza; but the
man responsible for making it famous was Shah
Fakhruddin of Delhi, who devoted many years to
serving the institution and taking it to great heights. He
ensured that his pupils passed on the knowledge of the
principles of conduct, obligatory and otherwise, based
on the Hadith to other students, thus starting a chain
of learning. The madrasa was *tassavwuf* (mysticism)-

oriented. Shah Fakhruddin was liberal enough to postulate the view that reading of *khutba* (Friday sermon) in Hindi was permissible so that it could reach the desired target. He had a magnetic personality and his scrupulous moral conduct was a byword in Delhi. The following story elucidates this: Shah Waliullah, Shah Fakruddin, and Mirza Mazhar Jan-e-Janan, three men of distinction, were once invited to dinner. The host, obviously wanting to test their patience, warmly welcomed them but retreated into the ladies' quarters on the pretext of bringing the food. After keeping the three august guests waiting for hours together, he came back empty-handed, asking to be excused on the pretext of his wife's illness. He then offered each of them a paltry amount of money instead. Shah Fakhruddin accepted the money standing, Shah Waliullah followed suit but remained seated, and Mirza Saheb accepted it with the remark: 'You have hurt me greatly.'

A study of its intellectual and cultural history convincingly shows that the years of Delhi's political decline, with the gradual waning of Mughal rule, in fact, saw a cultural and literary efflorescence. If historians were to assess Delhi's history in cultural and literary terms rather than political ones, they would indubitably perceive the Delhi of the 18th century to be a city at its most radiant rather than as a decaying metropolis. This

was a time when literary creativity in Urdu and free
thinking in religion gained momentum.

POLITICAL UPHEAVALS AND DELHI

The annals of Mughal Delhi are marked by calamity and
tragedy, pillage and destruction. A spate of invasions
followed the death of Alamgir and the weakening of the
central authority gave ascendancy to regional powers.
Shah Waliullah remarked pithily in this regard that
affairs in Delhi had been rendered as insignificant
as children at play, while it was a sitting target for
developments in other parts of the country. Any storm
arising from the Deccan would strike against the walls
of the Lal Qila; a dust storm from Punjab would shake
Delhi. Yet the nobles continued with their intrigues
while ensconced in the Red Fort. The history of the
Delhi of the 18th and 19th centuries is a long tale of
woe for its people. Nadir Shah attacked Delhi in 1739,
adding to the miseries of its citizens—each day bringing
new travails, each night a harbinger of darkness. Mirza
Jan-e Janan wrote in a letter:

از تشویشات ہر روزہ دہلی تنگ آمدہ ام۔

I dread the restless state in Delhi everyday.

Nadir Shah had turned Delhi into a pool of blood. Shaikh Mohammed Ashiq Phulti wrote in his *Alqaul-al Jali*:

They killed every living creature, human as well as animal, not sparing even the dogs and cats, besides setting homes and bazaars afire. There were stacks upon stacks of dead bodies. Rivers of blood flowed in the royal bazaar called Chandni Chowk. ... People in the thousands died of hunger and thirst; the foul smell of dead bodies caused an epidemic.

In stark contrast to the peaceful and tranquil Delhi of Shahjehan and Alamgir, Delhi was now a ghost city—of people struck by despondency, fright, lack of confidence and self-esteem, and paralysis of will. Left with no option but suicide, they decided to immolate themselves en masse. Shah Waliullah arrived as a saviour in this situation, imparting courage to the people by reminding them of the martyrdom of Hazrat Imam Husain. Nadir Shah's thirst, greed, and cruelty knew no bounds, driving people to madness, in the words of Harcharan Das. However, it was not the end of Delhi's woes, and repeated attacks by Ahmed Shah Abdali left another trail of blood and destruction. Delhi was being destroyed from within by intriguers and without by foreign assailants. The leading families of Delhi were the worst hit during the upheavals that deprived them of their livelihood and left them destitute. Mir draws this picture:

جس جا کہ خس و خار کے اب ڈھیر لگے ہیں

واں ہم نے انہی آنکھوں سے دیکھی ہیں بہاریں

یا قافلہ در قافلہ ان رستوں میں تھے لوگ

یا ایسے گئے یاں سے کہ پھر کھوج نہ پایا

سرسری تم جہاں سے گذرے

ورنہ ہر جا جہانِ دیگر تھا

اب خرابہ ہوا جہاں آباد

ورنہ ہر اک قدم پہ یاں گھر تھا

بے زری کا کر گلہ غافل

رہ تسلّی کہ یوں مقدر تھا

Mounds of dust and thorns are all that remain now,
Were those my own eyes that saw spring blossom?

Caravan after caravan of people was seen approaching,
But where have they all gone, leaving behind no trace?

Casually you passed by this world without bother
Though new worlds at each turn you could fathom.
Barrenness reigns where a living home was once
Do not complain of diminished means, you unwise person,
Console yourself saying it was writ in the stars.

The literature of that period presents a realistic portrayal of the chaos, disruption, and the trials and tribulations of the people. The painful conditions led the poets to express mourning and lamentation, pessimism and despair. Metaphors such as 'flower and nightingale', 'spring and autumn', and 'meeting and parting' were sometimes used by them as symbols for the harsh and bitter truths of contemporary social life. Poets such as Rafi Ahmed Sauda described the devastation in Delhi more directly. In his *Shahr Aasbhob*, he laments the lost glory of Delhi:

خراب ہیں وہ عمارات کیا کہوں تجھ پاس

کہ جن کے دیکھے سے جاتی رہے تھی بھوک اور پیاس

اور اب جو دیکھو تو دل ہوے زندگی سے اُداس

بجاے گُل، چمنوں میں کمر کمر ہے گھاس

کہیں ستون پڑا پڑا ہے، کہیں پڑے مرغول

In dilapidation lie the edifices, the mere sight
Of which sufficed to assuage hunger and thirst,
Now they leave the heart disillusioned with life,
Grass knee-high overgrown where flowers once bloomed
Broken pillars here, debris scattered everywhere.

However, even the vicissitudes of fate and trials and travails could not really dim the charms and attractions of Delhi for its inhabitants, and the poets and scholars of the city continually expressed their staunch loyalty to

it. As far back as during the time of Akbar, Shaikh Abdul
Haq Mohaddis had conveyed his unwillingness to leave
Delhi in a verse:

حقّی از گوشئہ دہلی نہ نہم پابیروں

خود گرفتم کہ ملک گجرا تم دادند

I will not leave this isolated corner of the city of Delhi
Even if I were given Gujarat to look after.

Mirza Bedil was not prepared to exchange it for the
entire world. He said, while rejecting Nizam-ul-Mulk's
invitation to come over to the Deccan: 'A world offered
will not make me move a bit, my contentment keeps
me as if myrtle-bound.' His couplet in this regard is as
follows:

دنیا اگر دہند، نہ جنبم زجائے خویش

من بستہ ام حنائے قناعت زپاے خویش

I will not budge from my place even if the world is offered to me
Just as if I have the henna of contentment painted on my feet.

Even when conditions deteriorated and it was difficult
to find livelihood in Delhi, nobody was prepared to leave
its streets and bylanes. The very idea of departure hurt
deeply and Zauq Ahmad Zauq spoke thus:

گرچہ ہے ملک دکن میں ان دنوں قدرِ سخن

کون جاے ذوقؔ پر دلّی کی گلیاں چھوڑ کر

Even though these days poesy beckons crowds to the Deccan,
O, Zauq, why would anyone leave the lanes of Delhi behind?

SPORTS AND ENTERTAINMENT

Sports and recreation featured prominently in the social life of Delhi from the 18th century onwards, with the scions of wealthy families in the prime of their youth being free of worry about the future. Almost every streetcorner, quadrangle, and open space was crowded with those wanting to spend their time watching cock fights and quail fights or flying kites or pigeons. These were favourite pastimes and indulgences of the young and old alike in Delhi. Of the youths' merrymaking, Mir said in a couplet:

کیا میرؔ تو روتا ہے پامالی دل ہی کو

ان لونڈوں نے تو دلّی سب سر پہ اُٹھا لی ہے

O Mir! Why bewail your broken heart
When urchins have made hell on Delhi's earth?

Delhi had regular kite-flying clubs. Kites of different shapes, sizes, and colours with interesting names such as *mangdar* (one with parted hair), *na'ldar* (like a horseshoe), and *kalejajali* (one with suffering heart) could be seen dotting the Delhi sky, swishing up from the sandy banks of the Jamuna. Mughal princesses were also fond of kite flying. Even in his last days, Emperor Bahadur Shah Zafar enjoyed watching this spectacle.

Another attraction of ordinary life in those days for common folk and courtiers alike was visiting the melas. Like other spheres of life, the fairs also reflected the impact of durbar life. However, as far as common people were concerned, lack of money and means often leads to immorality. Both Meena Bazaar and Kusal Bazaar were detrimental to social values. Moral dissolution in these fairs dated back to the time of Feroz Shah Tughlaq and continued into the 19th century. In fact, the melas were venues for carousal and wild merrymaking by vagabonds and people of low morals. *Murraqqa-e-Dehli* recorded that the Nagal ka Mela was held on the 27th day of every month, and women of easy virtue looking for fun would come dressed in enticing attire and stoop to vulgar conduct.

FESTIVALS

A special feature of Mughal Delhi was the bonhomie that existed between Hindus and Muslims who celebrated their festivals together. The Mughal emperors took the initiative for fostering this atmosphere of cordial coexistence, and the khaneqahs as well as bazaars contributed their share towards it. The emperors took special care of Hindu sensitivities on these occasions as the *Ain-i-Akbari* records. The death of Mariam Makani, Akbar's mother, plunged the durbar into mourning while Dussera was being celebrated. Akbar didn't want the festivities to be affected and, therefore, decided to cut short the period of mourning. He ordered his vizier, Shaikh Farid Nawab Murtaza Khan, to issue a royal farman to this effect.

Holi, Diwali, Salono, and Dussera were regularly celebrated at the Mughal durbar. Under Shah Alam II, Holi and Basant Panchami celebrations at the court were particularly colourful. Large crowds gathered near Qadam Sharif, and the surrounding orchards were full of milling crowds on these occasions. Qawwali sessions were organized and some mausoleums were the starting points of the Basant processions. Special arrangements were made at the mazars of Qutub Saheb, Shaikh Nizamuddin Aulia, Shaikh Nasiruddin Chirag-e Delhi, and Shah Hasan Rasulnuma for the Basant celebrations. Raksha Bandhan was celebrated by Akbar on a grand scale and Jehangir too kept this tradition alive. A large wooden effigy was burnt to mark the end of Dussera during the time of Jahandar Shah.

MUSHAIRAS (POETIC SYMPOSIA)

Mushairas were the heart and soul of the life of Delhi during the twilight years of the Mughal Empire. The fount of tradition was, of course, the Red Fort; the mansions of noblemen followed suit. The *diwan khana* (hall of audience) of every nobleman, the Chandni Chowk, and every qahwa khana at Chowk Saadullah were meeting places of poets and the literati. Famed for their repartee and spontaneous poetic creations, these gatherings used to be very interesting. The following anecdote highlights the poetic creativity of those times. It was the rainy season and Emperor Bahadur Shah Zafar was visiting Qutub Saheb, accompanied by members of his family. Mirza Fakhru and Zauq were also in attendance and both of them were enjoying the beauty of the moon's reflection upon the still water of a pond. It inspired Mirza Fakhru to come up with the line:

چاندنی دیکھے اگر وہ مہ جبیں تالاب پر

If that embodiment of the moon could watch the moon in the pond ...

Zauq was asked to complete the couplet. He came up with:

تابِ عکس رُخ سے پانی پھیر دے مہتاب پر

... she would pour water on the moon with her reflection.

The poetic get-togethers often generated heated exchanges and mutual rivalries that could turn sour. Adverse times also cast their shadow on these gatherings. Altaf Husain Hali writes about Ghalib's recital at a mushaira organized at the Diwan-e-Aam. It was almost daybreak when Ghalib's turn came. Tongue-in-cheek, Ghalib likened his recital to the singing of raga Bhairavi (the morning raga). First, he recited his Urdu verses as per the line given to him. Then he recited his soulful Persian verses poignantly. It seemed that few in the audience appreciated his verses. That's why he recited plaintively. Not meeting Ghalib in Delhi during the last phase of the Mughal Empire would be equivalent to committing a literary crime. Ghalib said:

دم از ریاست دہلی نمی زنم غالبّ

منم ز خاک نشینانِ آن دیار یکے

I am not talking of the kingdom of Delhi
I am one of the men sitting humbly in its dust.

Ghalib was, in fact, synonymous with the Delhi of his time. His way of life, humanism, and interests symbolized the soul of Delhi. He never had a house of his own and spent his days in rented houses at Gali Qasimjan or in the nearby Phatak Habash Khan. He also stayed for some time with Kale Saheb. Ghalib rarely lived in comfort and spent most of his life in destitution and anxiety. Often, he was troubled by the owner of the house where he was currently residing. To harass Ghalib, one owner erected wooden scaffolding, which Ghalib likened to gallows put up for a hanging. The rains would turn Gali Qasimjan into something like the canal of Saadat Khan. This was agony for his wife. The poet himself complained in a letter:

The door opening towards the veranda is dilapidated and the staircases are run-down. The chamber which is used for sitting in the morning has already sagged, its roof coming off. It rains briefly but the roof leaks for hours. Books and the ink stand are all in the storeroom, utensils scattered all over ... the *lagan* (copper pot) at one end and *chilamchi* (washbasin) at the other.

Yet this extreme poverty and hardship did not dim the light of inspiration and Ghalib always remained big-hearted and enlightened. Hali recalled: 'Disabled men and women were a common sight around his house and were ever-present before his eyes. But never would Ghalib turn a beggar away empty-handed.'

MUGHAL CULTURE

The greatest accomplishment of Mughal Delhi was its synthesis of Hindu and Muslim culture. The elite dressed alike and shared identical conduct and customs. A pictorial document, which is now in the library of the Windsor Palace in the UK, entitled *Badshahnama* contains a graphic account of the life of noblemen of the Mughal court. Not only was it difficult to distinguish a Hindu emir from a Muslim one, this was true of people from every rank of society. The Red Fort was not merely a centre of administration but a source of guidance in all aspects of city life. Any new style or custom starting from the fort would inevitably percolate down to the populace. Obviously, not everybody could build a Diwan-e-Aam, but every household of Delhi, both Hindu and Muslim, emulated life in the fort as best it could—whether in terms of celebrations for the birth of a child or on the occasion of a wedding or festivals. In the sphere of learning and literature too, Muslims and Hindus had similar tastes and interests. Both studied Hindi, Persian, and Urdu. In fact, there was a sharp spurt in the number of Hindu poets writing in Persian during the 17th century, while Muslims showed a flair for Hindi poetry. Abdur Rahim Khan-e Khana and Chandra Bhan Brahmin were products of this shared ethos. Nawab Mustafa Khan Shefta in his *Gulshan-e Bekhar* mentions as many as 61 Hindu poets writing in Urdu while Qutbuddin Batin in *Naghma-e Andaleeb* recorded the names of 80 Muslim poets who wrote in Hindi. As someone has put it beautifully:

Shahjehan has the same right over Urdu as an architect has over his artwork, and as long as Hindus and Muslims live they would remember him as a symbol of the matchless architecture of national integration. The masterpieces include the Taj Mahal and the Jama Masjid as also the Red Fort, but along with them stands the magnificent edifice of the Urdu language—a contribution dedicated to the generosity and full-heartedness of this great ruler.

This high tradition of religious tolerance, in essence, represented the finest in Mughal culture. On this, Durga Das, in his Persian work *Makhzan-ulAkhlaq*, has written:

The originator of all religions and beliefs is the Creator of the world who is the Sustainer of all the peoples. It is part of His scheme that every religion should have its own methodology and each one has received directions accordingly—the simile of an orchard having the genus of all kinds of plants and flowers. Thus, the Almighty enters the consciousness of the creatures in varied ways: in the case of a mosque, there is the call of Azan and there is the ringing of bells in a place of idol worship:

در حیر تم کہ دشمنیکفر و دیں چراست

ازیک چراغ کعبہ و بت خانہ روشن است

Amazed I am over the conflict of belief and unbelief when the Kaaba and the house of Idols are lit by the light of the same lamp.

Thus it is incumbent on all human beings to keep their hearts
pure ensuring that they treat each other as brothers.

These are not just empty words but represent the basic spirit of the Delhi of the time. When Nawab Dabir-ud-Daula Fariduddin Khan (the maternal grandfather of Sir Syed Ahmad Khan) distributed his estate just before his death, he gave a fair share of his property to his old diwan, Lala Tilok Chand.[9]

Hindus and Muslims passed the time of the day together in the same places of recreation. Prior to 1857, there used to be an archery club with a mixed membership. Sir Syed mentions a respected Hindu archer who would invariably invoke *Allaho Akbar* before shooting an arrow.[10] Even after having bid adieu to past glory and greatness, this most vital syncretic aspect of Delhi culture remained intact. Thus, the stock saying among the ulema was: 'Other cities are like slave girls and Delhi is the queen.' Similarly, 'They are empty shells whereas Delhi is a pearl.'

[9] *Seerat-e Fareediya* (account of Fariduddin Khan [Minister of Akbar Shah Saani]), published by Sir Syed Ahmad Khan from Matba-e Mufid-e Aam, Agra, 1886, p. 38. Khaliq Anjum has also published *Seerat-e Faridia*, AnjumanTaraqqi Urdu (Hind), New Delhi.

[10] *Seerat-e Fareediya*, p. 4.

Elegies to Delhi written soon after 1857 do not mourn so much the eclipse of the Mughal Empire as they do the decimation of the civilizational ethos of the time. Until 1857, Mughal Delhi, despite the waning of Mughal might, was able to retain its basic cultural fabric. The Lal Qila stood outwardly the same as it was in the time of Shahjehan. Yet its old magnificence and grandeur had faded away. Hallowed spots where not a winged creature could venture were now repositories of the droppings of pigeons and bats. The emperor lived on doles from the East India Company (hereafter the Company), and for a mere pittance of an increase in his pension he had to submit application after application to the resident. Most of the royal princes, known as sultans, faced starvation, so much so that by the time of Akbar Shah II, these princes would climb on their rooftops crying out: 'We are dying of hunger.' Sauda paints a pathetic picture of their plight and humiliation:

مجا رکھی ہے سلاطینوں نے یہ توبہ دھاڑ

کوئی تو گھر سے نکل آئے ہیں گریباں پھاڑ

کوئی در اپنے پہ آ، دے دے مارتا ہے کواڑ

کوئی کہے، جو ہم ایسے ہی چھاتی کے ہیں پہاڑ

The sultans are raising a furore about their woes,
Some storm out of their abodes with lapels torn.
While others bang and break down their doors,

Still others cry, 'If on your chests we are burdens
Then better administer us poisoned potions.'

In fact, the sultans were not even allowed to stir out
of their houses and look for jobs. After managing to
escape from the fort, Azfari described in his memoirs
the strict restraints placed on them, with watchmen as
well as watchwomen having been posted to keep their
movements under surveillance. 'The begum in charge
of the palace deputed women to visit the houses of the
sultans. In whatever condition we would be in, they
would come many times during the day and night to
check on us with their own eyes and give their reports
to the begum.'

In *Bazm-e-Akhir*, Munshi Faiyazuddin recorded the
hollowness of the surviving grand traditions of two
kings of Delhi: Akbar Shah II and Bahadur Shah Zafar.
Drums still sounded at the Naqqarkhana, and farmans
and edicts were issued from the Darul Inshah, but
they had no more authority than a child's make-believe
games. The orders were not acted upon even within the
precincts of the fort, let alone beyond it. Yet, the writ
of the durbar still held sway in the social and cultural
spheres of the city in the way festivals were celebrated
and poetic and literary symposia were held with the
basic guiding principle being syncreticism. Navroz,
Shab-e-barat, Madar Chari, Moharram, Holi, Salono,

and Dussehra were celebrated as of old; festivals such
Giarvin Sharif (birth of Shah Abdul Qadir Jeelani) were
also observed. The Phoolwalon-ki-Sair (the festival of
flowers) was taken out in a spirit of harmony. Ghalib
noted: 'Life in Delhi is based on several things: the
Qila, Chandni Chowk, the bazaar at Jama Masjid every
day, the picnic on the Jamuna every week, and the
Phoolwalon-ki-Sair once a year.'

The events of 1857 upset this rhythm. The fort
turned into a prison, Chandni Chowk and Khanam
Bazaar lay barren, Jama Masjid was padlocked, Masjid
Akbarabadi was razed to the ground, and the khaneqahs
turned into ruins while madrasas became agricultural
fields. Prominent families faced destruction and their
members found it difficult to keep their honour intact.
People were left with no choice but to start moving out
of the city. Lights went out at the khaneqah of Shah
Ghulam Ali and Madrasa Rahimia wound up. Ghalib
wrote of this:

A large deserted expanse from Jama Masjid to Rajghat
sprawls, and if the heaps of bricks are cleared what would
be left is an empty void. ... From the Kabuli Darwaza to the
Kalkata Darwaza lies an open field ... no trace of many famous
havelis, mansions, Punjabi Katra, Dhobiwada, Ramji Ganj,
Katra Saadat Khan, Haveli Jernail, houses of Ramjidas, Saheb
Rambagh. By God! Delhi is no more a city but an army camp,
or a cantonment. ... No fort, no bazaar, no city.

This was not just the end of an empire but of an entire civilization where the exalted values of Indian culture had been nurtured. Those witnessing the devastation cried out in distress:

تذکرہ دلی مرحوم کا اے دوست نہ چھیڑ

نہ سُنا جائے گا ہم سے یہ فسانہ ہرگز

O friend, mention the tale of the deceased Delhi,
I don't have the heart to hear this sorry tale.

3

Ghalib's Delhi

....

Like the personality and thoughts of Ghalib, the history of Delhi had two distinct periods. The events of 1857 caused a dramatic break from the past for Delhi and its inhabitants. In its 800-year-long history, Delhi had changed its form many times—Siri, Kilokeri, Tughlaqabad, Ferozabad, and Shahjehanabad to name but a few of its incarnations—but each was an added layer which seamlessly connected with the past. The events of 1857 shattered the historical links with the past and Delhi was, as English poet Matthew Arnold has said in a different context, 'wandering between two worlds, one dead the other powerless to be born'. Ghalib too suffered the tribulations of Delhi. The old Delhi was breathing its last and the new had not yet been conceived. The Ghalib from before 1857 was entirely different from the one after it. For the inhabitants of Delhi, it was difficult to make sense of a present that bore no relation to the recent past. Ghalib opens up his wounds to friends thus:

Saheb, do you understand what the matter is and what has happened? That was a birth when both of us were friends and there was an exchange of love and affection in our dealings with each other. Together we recited our poetry, compiled our works ... suddenly the times changed; no more were those friends, that cordiality, mutual discourse, happiness. Afterwards there was the rebirth, albeit the forms of the two were exactly the same. That is, the city where I am bears the name of Delhi and the locality of Ballimaran is also the same, but I do not find the friends of my earlier birth.[1]

A man who speaks of two births still sees Mir Mahdi climbing up staircases and hears the echo of Yusuf Mirza's voice.[2] This was the psyche of a man of deep sensitivity assailed by a social typhoon upsetting the very purpose of his life. The slings of outrageous fortune turned Ghalib into an elegy personified:

منحصر مرنے پہ ہو جس کی اُمّید

ناامیدی اس کی دیکھا چاہیے

ہوچکیں، غالب! بلائیں سب تمام

ایک مرگِ ناگہانی اور ہے

[1] A letter to Mirza Hargopal Tafta of Sikandrabad, 5 December 1857, in Khaliq Anjum, ed., *Ghalib ke Khutoot*, Ghalib Institute, New Delhi, 1984, pp. 266–7.

[2] A letter to Mir Sarfaraz Husain, 1858, in Khaliq Anjum, ed., *Ghalib ke Khutoot*, Ghalib Institute, New Delhi, 1985, p. 762.

One whose only hope is to die,
Fathom the state of his desperation!
O Ghalib, your disasters are done with,
What remains is your sudden death.

The decimation of Delhi resulted not only in the destruction of the political order but also marked the end of a civilization and the annihilation of an ethical structure nurtured jointly by Hindus and Muslims for some 300 years. Poets had once written satirical laments about Delhi, but now was the time to write its elegy. What Khusrau had described as Revered Delhi (Hazrat-e Dehli), a sanctuary of religion and justice, was now 'Deceased Delhi'. A poet breathing in such a claustrophobic atmosphere was bound to feel completely hopeless. Before 1857, Delhi was an integral part of Ghalib's personality, but the Delhi of later years was a graveyard of lost hopes. Ghalib's own relationship with the Mughal court had been beset with a thousand complications, but he was still attached to the heart of Delhi. The last Mughal ruler had indeed been a helpless man, although in the eyes of the common people, the fort remained a symbol and a focal point around which the city's culture and its aspirations flourished. After 1857, the same Ghalib who had once lived with honour and some contentment, despite facing hardships, could be seen knocking at the doors of nawabs and ingratiating himself with English officers.

In the words of Maulana Abul Kalam Azad, it was an irony that a person like Ghalib, who was so proud of his art, was forced to make submissions before a greenhorn officer with his head bowed in acquiescence.[3] Ghalib had once incurred a debt of 40,000–50,000 rupees but it was then a symbol of his status and he had enough self-confidence to turn down the advice of Nasikh to go over to Hyderabad for employment at the Deccan Court. But now Ghalib's patience gave out when he ran into a debt of a mere 800 rupees. He exhausted himself making humble submissions before the nawab of Rampur. A man who had thought it beneath his dignity to accept office under Bahadur Shah was now saying:

وہ دن گئے جو کہتے تھے "نوکر نہیں ہوں میں

Gone are the days when I used to say, 'I am no one's servant.'

He was now telling Kalb-e Ali Khan with humility and helplessness:

خیرات خوارِ محض ہوں نوکر نہیں ہوں میں

I live merely on doles, not that I am even a servant.[4]

[3] Ateeq Siddiqui, *Ghalib aur Abul Kalam*, 1969, p. 202.

[4] I dwell at the house of Kalb-e Ali Khan / I do not live by begging from door to door / O Asad! I am now old and

In such a ruthless times, the weight of circumstances
burdened the shoulders of a sensitive poet such as
Ghalib. He could not help saying with a heavy heart:

اے تازہ واردانِ بساط ہوا ے دل

زنہار! اگر تمہیں ہوس ناے و نوش ہے

دیکھو مجھے جو دیدۂ عبرت نگاہ ہو

میری سنو، جو گوش نصیحت نیوش ہے

O new arrivals in the realm of the heart,
Beware the yearning for wine and the arts.
Observe me and be warned if you are wise,
And be prepared if you are to heed my advice.

The decline of Mughal rule began in the 18th
century and by the dawn of the 19th century, the
Mughal emperor was no more than a figurehead.
However, political decline and the resulting instability
and withdrawal of patronage had not stopped literary
and intellectual development in society. On the face
of it, this may look like a contradiction, but it is true
that instability and churning give rise to great literature
and philosophical thought. Compton-Ricket assessed
English literary and intellectual movements and wrote,

---

decrepit, I can't run errands / I live merely on doles, not that
I am even a servant.

'The great flowering of English Renaissance was not the moment when Drake and Hawkins were defying Philip of Spain. After the defeat of the Armada came the triumph of Shakespeare.'[5]

If it is true that defeat of the Armada led to the flowering of Shakespeare's thoughts and skills, it would not be far from the truth to assert that the intellectual giants among the Muslims of India rose to prominence at the time of the sunset of Mughal rule. Shah Waliullah, Ghalib, and Sir Syed were the products of this age of political decline. The society that gave birth to them was undeniably still full of robust moral and intellectual potential. Shah Waliullah's Madrasa Rahimia was the fountain of knowledge and academic excellence when the Battle of Plassey was under way in Bengal. The madrasa run by Shah Waliullah enjoyed unparalleled fame as a centre of learning. The highly acclaimed works of Ghazali, Razi, and Ibn-e-Rushd were eclipsed by the works of Shah Waliullah, if one were to quote Maulana Shibli Nomani.[6]

Shah Waliullah stood tall in terms of erudition amongst all other scholars of Islam over its 900-year

[5] Arthur Compton Rickett, *A History of English Literature*, 1912, p. 680.

[6] Shibli Nomani, *Ilmul Kalam*, Dar-ul Anwar-ul Matabar, Lucknow, p. 117.

history. The decline of the Mughal Empire, in a strange contradiction, was accompanied by a wave of cultural, scholastic, and intellectual resurgence, manifesting itself in the genius of Shah Abdul Aziz, Syed Ahmed Shahid, Shah Mohammed Ismail, Ghalib, Sir Syed, Maulana Mamluk Ali, Mufti Sadruddin Azurda, and Momin.

The Delhi of Ghalib was one that nurtured the founders of the magnificent institutions of Deoband, Aligarh, and Nadwa. Ghalib's poetry evolved in such a centre of erudition and blossomed in an ambience of initial interface between the East and the West. The Delhi College was the forerunner and initiator of this new age. The history of Delhi witnessed two occasions when the ulema of Delhi were frontrunners among the ulema of the Islamic world: first, after the havoc wreaked by the Tartars, when Delhi had great scholars of the same stature as Razi and Ghazali.[7]

The historian Arnold Toynbee, in the course of discussing the decline and fall of civilizations, said that new cultural trends surface when the 'schism of the soul' and the 'schism of the body politic' peak and lead on to the emergence of some personalities who are capable of finding ways of progress and reawakening out of decline. Times of adversity are catalysts of renewal

[7] Khaleeq Ahmad Nizami, *Tareekh-e Maqalat*, Delhi, 1966, p. 212.

and progress. Ghalib's Delhi was reflective of a cultural upsurge. We often fail to comprehend that the death of an old way of life carries within itself seeds of renewal and reconstruction that are necessary for overcoming the decay of the old. Prone as we are to understanding history only in terms of political developments and the rise and decline of empires, we often miss out on the other aspects of life in an age.

In the eyes of Ghalib, the entire hustle and bustle in Delhi was centred on five features: the Red Fort, Chandni Chowk, the Jama Masjid, the Jamuna, and Phoolwalon-ki-Sair.[8] They were the pivots of social and cultural life in Delhi, as also the pivot of Ghalib's feelings and emotions.

The *qila* (fort) was the heart of the social and cultural life of Delhi. From the very time of Shahjehan, people living around the qila were connected to the durbar in one way or other. It enjoyed a central position in their lives. They made efforts to imitate the life of the qila and decorated their houses accordingly. The qila had a Diwan-e-Aam and a Diwan-e-Khas. Like the Diwan-e-Aam and Diwan-e-Khas, the houses of the affluent had diwan khanas and those of the less well off had *mardaney* (exclusively for male visitors), whereas poorer people

---

[8] Ghalib's letter to Mir Mahdi Majruh, 2 December 1851, in Anjum, *Ghalib ke Khutoot*, p. 514.

had *baithaks* or sitting rooms. Evidently, economic conditions were no barrier for people attempting to follow the trends of the age set by the court.

Delhi became the chosen target of adventurers: a storm arising from the Deccan would eventually strike Lal Qila; a dust storm passing over Punjab would buffet Delhi. The English forces entered Delhi under the command of General Lake in 1803 reducing the Mughal king to an employee of the Company. They were in no haste and worked out their strategy behind a smokescreen. Thus, instead of directly removing the king, they decided to consolidate power without overt hostility to Bahadur Shah, who had turned 62 on ascending the throne in 1857. He was a man of many great qualities that his immediate predecessors had lacked, but he was not strong enough to shoulder the heavy responsibilities of office. During that time, Delhi was the country's Weimar, as Spear has put it, and Ghalib was its Goethe.[9] The qila was like an illusion obstructing a clear view of the reality.

The walls and gates of the fort that had witnessed such glory during the reign of Shahjehan were still intact. The edifice, as usual, cast its reflection upon the Jamuna and everything in the durbar was overtly the same: maroon-

[9] Percival Spear, *Twilight of the Mughals: Studies in Late Mughal Delhi*, Cambridge University Press, 1951, p. 73.

coloured curtains hung in the fort as in Shahjehan's time, glittering robes and jewellery were on display, money continued to be distributed among the poor like in the olden days, and Bahadur Shah still received a gun salute when going out of the fort. All this was, nonetheless, no more than an illusion. The banks of the Jamuna, once the venue of elephant fights, had turned into an arena for quail fights and kite flying. What Adam Mez said of Baghdad before its decline in his *Renaissance of Islam* was true of the Delhi of Bahadur Shah Zafar. Where once strategies of wars and battles in the fields of Badakhshan and Kandahar used to be chalked out, there were now petty rivalries and fights between the royals. The princes of Delhi erstwhile lived in nine mansions, but now they were living on borrowed time and money. Fortunes of many a nobleman and governor had been made and destroyed in these mansions, but now only strategies on how to get loans from moneylenders were drawn up there and bribes demanded of job-seekers. In Jahangir's *Tuzuk* (memoirs), there is mention of the practice of *nazrana* (offerings) payment required of noblemen to be paid to the royal treasury, which was perhaps an effective strategy for putting restrictions on their ever-growing wealth. Things had now come to such a pass that the grant of positions was made a tool for extorting money. Bahadur Shah drew a pension of 1 lakh rupees, and that was hardly enough for meeting his expenses, considering his extravagant ways. An insight into the ageing emperor's mind can be gained from the following newspaper reports:

Report of 28 August 1846. Rahimuddin and Abdullah presented themselves in the durbar, each offering one rupee and two packets of sweets, along with the request to be accepted as *murids* (spiritual disciples) of the king. The request granted, the king gave them discourses on matters of theology and spiritual love, and a handkerchief and rosary each before they left.[10]

The fondness for leading people in matters of religion was not new. Akbar had preferred to give fishing hooks to his new disciples on the occasion of their pledging allegiance to him. But it was a pastime for him, whereas Bahadur Shah took it seriously, perhaps as an escape from the ruthlessness of the times.

Report of 24 September 1847. On the occasion of the rakhi mela, His Majesty gave 50,000 rupees to Raja Bholanath and one gold coin to his palanquin carriers. Amid celebrations, His Majesty chose a maiden, a Venus-like beauty, as his bride and honoured her by making her one of the royal consorts. He conferred upon her the title of Akhtar Mahal and granted her a eunuch and two guards, besides jewellery of high value in large quantity.[11] As Khawaja Hasan Nizami noted, even in

[10] *Ahsan-ul Akhbar*, in Hasan Nizami, comp., *Dehli ki Akhree Sans*, Halka-e Mashayak, Delhi, p. 93.

[11] *Ahsan-ul Akhbar*, p. 186.

his old age, the Emperor's fondness for marriage remained young.

Report of 15 October 1847. The revered emperor of Shajahenabad watched and enjoyed the spectacle of quail fights.[12]

Marriage in advanced years, the desire to be a spiritual guide, and fondness for watching quail fights are hardly the qualities of a good king. However, it would be unfair to see them in isolation and overlook their connection with public life. The emperor spent most of the grant he was getting for personal expenses for keeping alive the traditions linking him with the masses than on himself. Of course, the people of Delhi were very fond of him. Be it an occasion of happiness or sorrow, he was on hand to extend help and sympathy in cash or kind; in times of natural calamity the emperor would personally attend to relief work. The fact of the matter was that if the emperor was a prisoner of the Company on the one hand, he remained bound by the great traditions of the Timur clan on the other. The Company kept his hands tied, but the hard realization of his inability to measure up to the ancestral traditions indeed made him shed tears of blood.

Ghalib was a frequent visitor to the durbar; but at the same time, he got monetary favours from the Governor General as well. This was the bitter reality of the times.

[12] *Ahsan-ul Akhbar*, p. 191.

When Ghalib was arrested on charges of gambling and
the emperor wrote a letter recommending his release,
attributing the charge to a 'mischief' on the part of
those nursing a grudge against a respectable citizen,[13]
Nawab Saheb Kalan replied that a court case was already
pending in the matter, and the law did not brook any
intervention. If the people had come to know that a
successor of Akbar and Jehangir had had his request
turned down by any authority, it would have been a bitter
pill to swallow. The powerless emperor spent most of
his time paying visits to the dargah of Qutub Saheb and
strolling in its neighbourhood, not for recreation but
to drive away thoughts of his powerlessness that were
eating into him. Although he remained a respected
figurehead for the people, his impotence was evident.
Ghalib might have spoken often of his 'washing the
feet of the king of sweet poetry' but he too fully grasped
the meaning of the bitter reality of the durbar having
become a body without soul. The following couplet by
Ghalib captures the helpless state of Bahadur Shah:

بازیچۂ اطفال ہے، دنیا مرے آگے

ہوتا ہے شب و روز تماشا مرے آگے

The world is only a child's play for me,
Night and day, a spectacle goes on in front of me.

[13] *Ahsan-ul Akhbar,* p. 171.

Jama Masjid was central to the Mughal period, just like Hauz-e-Shamsi had been in earlier times. It was a meeting place for men of letters, ulema, scholars and writers, Sufis and poets, as well as pleasure seekers and idlers. It was a hub for preachers and storytellers, healers selling fancy drugs, literary sessions and poetry, unending rounds of buying and selling. *Muraqqua-e Dehli*[14] gives a graphic account of the scene around Jama Masjid of those days. Shah Abu Said Mujaddi proclaimed a fatwa against the English from the steps of the Jama Masjid,[15] Shah Mohammad Ismail spoke from its pulpit. The voices emanating from its stairs reverberated across the city.

Shahjehan had planned the fort in such a way that it looked like a rose stretching out its petals: the Jama Masjid, with its minarets kissing the sky, faced arterial roads running in different directions with shops and markets on both sides; the canal running up to Chandni Chowk lent beauty to the surroundings. Every market was known for its speciality—Khas Bazaar, Urdu Bazaar,

[14] Nawab Zulqadr Quli Khan, *Muraqqua-e Dehli*, Taj Press, Hyderabad; Urdu translations available as Nurul Hasan, *Muraqqa-e Dehli*, Delhi University, 1982; Khaliq Anjum, ed. and trans., *Muraqqa-e Dehli*, New Delhi, 1993.

[15] Abdul Latif, *1857 ka Tareekhi Roz Namcha*, pp. 88–9.

and Khanam Bazaar.[16] In Khanam Bazaar, for example, were shops of jewellers and stone setters. Behind the Jama Masjid were shops selling spices and pulses while opium vendors did business on the upper floors. Below its steps to the south were retail shops selling different items, while on the steps to the north were shops selling firecrackers. Apart from the main bazaars, every lane had shopping and business centres—Ballimaran was known for its ironmongers, Kucha Pundit for bangles, butchers were located in Kucha Saadullah. The populace and the city as a whole were divided into mohallas, lanes and bylanes, squares, katras, havelis, and *mandi*s (bazaars, mainly wholesale). The scheme was somewhat different from that of Daulatabad in the time of Mohammad bin Tughlaq, where each part of the city was earmarked for one particular section of people, as observed by the author of *Subh-ul-Asha*, Aḥmad bin 'Alī al-Qalqashandī. No such arrangement was ever seen again.

It is surprising that unlike in the case of Medina, Damascus, and Baghdad, whose histories had been

---

[16] In a letter to Abdul Ghafoor Surur, penned in September 1860, Ghalib wrote, 'It seems as if the entire city is being demolished. Now one can't even have the trace of big markets such as Nami Bazaar, Khas Bazaar, Urdu Bazaar, and Khanam Bazaar, although every bazaar constituted a small town' (Anjum, *Ghalib ke Khutoot*, p. 607).

compiled early during the medieval era, nobody thought of writing a history of Delhi until Sir Syed and Sangeen Beg[17] did in the 19th century. A sociological survey shows that the city of Delhi had certain areas named after viziers, noblemen, et cetera, but most localities were named after the vocations of craftsmen and artisans inhabiting the area—cloth merchants, bangle and soap sellers, weavers, et cetera. Thus, there were and are names such as Choori-walan, Kaghazion ka Mohalla, Jauhari Bazaar, Bazazon ka Katra, and Mamaron ka Chhatta.

In those times, diwankhanas hosting mehfils of poets and littérateurs were a central feature of Delhi's social life. Maulana Azad correctly pointed out that this was the last phase in Delhi's literary and intellectual history spanning 700 years. Significantly, the evening sessions attended by intellectuals were like the salons in Europe which were foundries that shaped new ways of thinking and literature. Sir Syed wrote about the diwan khana of Maulana Sadruddin Azurda: 'The discussions evoke memories and bring tears to the eyes, the get-togethers of the past are mere remembrances.'[18]

[17] Mirza Sangeen Baig, *Sair-ul Manaazil*, ed. and trans. into Urdu by Sharif Husain Qasmi, Ghalib Institute, New Delhi, 1982.

[18] *Tasaneef-e Ahmadiya*, Part I, p. 136.

Maulana Azad's father recited an Arabic verse, remembering the sittings at diwankhanas with tears welling up in his eyes: 'Do enjoy fully the spring-time of Nejd, it won't last beyond evening.'[19]

تمتع من شميم عراد نجد

فما بعد العشيد من عراد

The diwankhanas of Sehbai, Momin, Azurda, Nayyer, Ashraf, and Hasrati were cradles of literature and scholarship. In fact, the home of every scholar and nobleman was a centre of learning and every lane and alley was a meeting place for the exchange of ideas and for discussions.

Sir Syed has quoted from an Arabic poem of Shah Abdul Aziz's in *Aasar-us-Sanadid*:

يا من يسائل من دهلى و رفعتها

على البلاد و ما حازتم من شرف

ان البلاد اماء و هى سيّدة

و انها درة و الكل كالصدف

فيها مدارس لوطاف البصير بها

لم تنفتح عينه الاعلى الصحف

---

[19] Siddiqui, *Ghalib aur Abul Kalam*, p. 187.

> *O the man asking about the conditions in Delhi, and*
> *Of other cities that match its accomplishments, listen!*
> *Doubtless the city of Delhi is the master and leader*
> *While other metropolises are but mere slaves to it,*
> *Delhi is the pearl, while others just (empty) shells,*
> *So many madrasas do there exist, and one who*
> *Takes a round would find books and books alone.*[20]

The khaneqahs and madrasas were indeed packed with books, and every nobleman had a library of his own. Those who could not afford to buy books or those who, like Ghalib, were not fond of buying them, borrowed them.[21]

It was difficult to count the numbers of madrasas, khaneqahs, and mosques in Delhi of those times. There was a madrasa at every step, a mosque and khaneqah in every street. According to Sadat Yar Khan Rangeen, Nawab Najabat Khan, who was given a large piece of property by Lord Lake, was said to have either built or repaired some 200 mosques.[22] The number of spots within the Jama Masjid area where Tarawih prayers were held during the month of Ramadan is simply astounding.

[20] Sir Syed, *Aasar-us Sanadid*, p. 522.

[21] Hali, *Yadgar-e Ghalib*, p. 17.

[22] *Akhbar-e Rangeen*, pp. 61–2.

The khaneqah of Hazrat Shah Ghulam Ali was, as poet Hali put it, the shelter and refuge of the faithful.[23] It attracted pilgrims from places as far away as China, Egypt, Syria, and Ethiopia who, after receiving training, went back to their countries for propagation and preaching. As for people from within the country and neighbouring nations, Sir Syed wrote: 'People from other places in the country and Punjab and Afghanistan throng this khaneqah.'[24]

Shah Ghulam Ali was a saint of exceptional popularity and repute. None in the country equalled his influence across foreign lands.

Shah Mohammed Afaque's mausoleum was another place that drew a large number of devotees. Maulana Fazl-ur-Rehman Ganj Moradabadi once told Maulana Mohammed Ali Mongiri, founder of Nadwat-ul-Ulema: 'I have seen two shops of love—one of Shah Ghulam Ali and the other of Shah Mohammed Afaque. People came to buy "love" from here.'[25] Both of them are located in

[23] Altaf Husain Hali, *Hayat-e Jawid*, Taraqqi-e Urdu Bureau, New Delhi, 1982 [1901], p. 303; English translation available as *Hayat-e Javed: A Biography of Sir Sayyid*, trans. David Mathews, Rupa & Co., New Delhi, 1994.

[24] Sir Syed, *Aasar-us Sanadid*.

[25] *Fazl-e Rahmani*, Malfuzat of Maulana Fazl-ur Rahman Ganj Moradabadi, p. 29.

Delhi. Today it is difficult to comprehend the meaning of 'shop of love' because the world that understood the meaning of 'shop of love' is no more. Ghalib would not have visited these 'shops' but would have been aware of their universal appeal.

The khaneqahs of Kale Saheb, Khwaja Nasir, Shah Ghayasuddin Chishti, Shah Sabir Husain, and Mir Mohammedi[26] were centres of education and instruction. Sir Syed's references to some of them in *Aasar-us-Sanadid* make it possible for us to assess their import as well as their sphere of influence. King and beggar alike were emotionally attached to them. Bahadur Shah, like Ghalib, had deep affection for and faith in Kale Saheb.

The madrasas of Shah Abdul Aziz, Shah Abdul Qadir, and Shah Rafiuddin attracted pilgrims from everywhere. Shah Abdul Aziz ascended the pulpit of his illustrious father, Shah Waliullah, when he was 17 years old and dispensed knowledge and learning for the next 60 years. Maulana Obaidullah Sindhi was of the opinion that Shah Abdul Aziz outshone Shah Waliullah in respect of number of disciples. If Shah Waliullah had 10 disciples, Shah Abdul Aziz had 10,000.[27] Sir Syed paid him tribute in the highest terms, saying that as long as

[26] *Mukhtasar Halaat ke Liye, Tareekhi Maqalat*, pp. 225–31.

[27] Maulana Obaidullah Sindhi, *Shah Waleeullah aur Unki Siyasee Tahreek*, Lahore, 1945, p. 64.

the Shah was alive it was hardly possible for anyone else to claim himself a scholar.

Shah Abdul Qadir lived in Masjid Akbrabadi,[28] which became the focal point for the revolutionary movement in 1857 and was later destroyed by the English who razed it to the ground, leaving no trace of it. Writing about Shah Waliullah, Iqbal points to the streak of modernity in his thought. His successors, realizing the need of the times, switched over to Urdu as the medium of instruction for religious teachings. The Shah Abdul Aziz School occupied a pivotal place in Ghalib's Delhi, and its exponents—Maulvi Rashiduddin Khan, Maulana Makhsoosullah, Abdul Hai, Mohammed Ishaq, Nawab Qutbuddin Khan, and Mamluk-ul-Ala—were pillars of knowledge. Their madrasas were centres of exegetical studies. If, on the one hand, illustrious alumni of Deoband such as Rasheed Ahmad Gangohi and Mohammed Qasim Naunatwi were trained under the preceptorship of Maulanas Makhsoosullah and Mamluk Ali, there was also, on the other hand, Sir Syed Ahmad Khan, founder of the Aligarh College. The conventional educational system had potential despite its many failings. Its critics only saw the drawbacks of traditional syllabi. They failed to consider its innate potential that moulded the personality and built character.

[28] *Waqa-e Abdul Qadir Khani*, p. 216.

The most important movement of pre-1857 Delhi was that of Maulana Syed Ahmad Shaheed. It fired the imagination of the entire country from Bala Kot to Calcutta. Even a poet such as Momin, who was prepared to 'crawl prostrate down the lane of his rival in love' suddenly stood up saying:

الٰہی مجھے شہادت نصیب

یہ افضل سے افضل عبادت نصیب

الٰہی اگرچہ میں ہوں تیرہ کار

پہ تیرے کرم کا ہوں امیدوار

تو اپنی عنایت سے توفیق دے

عروج شہید اور صدیق دے

God, do grant me the honour of martyrdom,
Distinction of distinctions of highest worship.
God, dark deeds I did commit, yet await your Mercy.
With kindness do give me the ability to reach
The pinnacle of martyrdom and truthfulness.

How did the various movements impact Ghalib? We are given an insight into his state of mind when he says:

ایمان مجھے روکے ہے جو کھینچے ہے مجھے کفر

کعبہ میرے پیچھے ہے، کلیسا میرے آگے

Belief stops me, unbelief beckons me:
I have Kaaba behind me and the church in front.

This verse expresses his mental state, which was unavoidable in those circumstances.

Like the Persian poet Urfi, Ghalib also 'went to the gate of the temple in the shadow of his faith', and had an excuse for drinking wine before God:

حساب مے و رامش و رنگ و بو

زجمشید و بہرام و پرویز جو

کہ از بادہ تا چہرہ افروختند

دل دشمن و چشم بد سوختند

نہ از من کہ از ناب مے گاہ گاہ

بدریوزہ رخ کردہ باشم سیاہ

جہاں از گل و لالہ پر بوئے و رنگ

من و حجرہ و دامنے زیر سنگ

Oh, call to account Jamshid Begram as also Pervez
For drinking wine and indulging in the worldly ways.
My face, aglow from the wine, burns the rival's heart.
Occasional wine blackens my begrudging foe's visage
Roses and tulips lend the world colour and fragrance
My own abode is humble, strewn with hard stones.

Ghalib's waywardness had won the heart of Ghaus Ali Shah, and he was impressed by his humility and unwillingness to harm anybody. Ghalib was no Sufi, nor could he be one, but his *qalandari* (from *qalandar*, one who is not bothered about wordly affairs or the repurcussions of his actions/nature) indifference had a touch of Sufi thinking.

Delhi was a city of sunlight and shade. There was ample space in it for asceticism as well as epicureanism. *Murraqqa-e Dehli* gives an account of mohallas given over entirely to pleasure and revelry. In the time of Mohammed bin Tughlaq, these places of entertainment were known as *tarbabad* (abodes of pleasure). At other times, they turned into dens of debauchery—with prostitutes and gamblers—as happens during times of despondency and pessimism, according to historian Arnold Toynbee. The weakening of Mughal rule affected the social, economic, and cultural life of Delhi as its denizens knew it. New social ideas started taking shape and new economic classes sprung up. Old businesses wound up and old trades on which families had depended for livelihood started becoming redundant. Thanks to his poetic insight, Ghalib understood the importance of change and chose to compromise with the changing times. Asked by Sir Syed to write an introduction for an Urdu translation of the *Ain-e-Akbari*, Ghalib broke away from the cultural heritage which he was steeped in. He played down the achievements of Akbar in comparison to those of the British. Obviously, this was not Ghalib's real opinion but only reflected his decision to make a compromise with the circumstances.[29] He was once again in the situation where he had to fold his hands before Nawab Kalb-e Ali Khan and say, 'I abide by the command of Allah and withdraw myself from the investigation.'[30]

Despite its economic decline and social disintegration, Delhi retained the cultural richness of a heritage jointly built by Hindus and Muslims. Festivals and carnivals were celebrated with great pomp and show, and its clubs were unparalleled. Sir Syed had spent a lot of time in his early life in the clubs of Delhi, of which both Hindus and Muslims were members. Hali wrote about his outings to parks and gardens, concerts of music, and feasts. He also attended the celebrations for Holi and the Phoolwalon-ki-Sair processions. Basant celebrations were organized at the home of a respected Muslim savant, Khwaja Mohammed Ashraf, who also attended events held at the house of Rai Pran Kishan.[31] There were clubs for kite

[29] He writes: 'If you speak in terms of law and constitution, open your eyes and look at the English people amid these ancient surroundings. Watch them intently, observe their etiquettes. They deserve to write the constitution. None can run the country better than they.'

[30] Siddiqui, *Ghalib aur Abul Kalam*, p. 203.

[31] *Hayat-e Jawed*, p. 54.

flying, archery, and swimming attended by Hindus and Muslims alike. Rangeen mentions archer Gulab Singh who invoked *Allaho Akbar* before shooting an arrow.[32]

People gathered on the banks of the Jamuna for swimming during summers and the rainy season. Sir Syed wrote:

My elder brother and I took swimming lessons from our father. There was a time when the famous swimmer Maulvi Aleemullah would lead a group of swimmers including Mirza Mughal and Mirza Taghal, famous swimmers of their time; the other was the group of my father accompanied by 125 of his pupils. All would jump into the river together, and this whole lot would go swimming from Majnu ka tila to the left bank of Shaikh Mohammed.[33]

Some batches of swimmers would gather at a point near Zinat-ul-Masajid in the orchard of Nawab Ahmed Baksh and continue to swim in the river till evening prayers. Even though Ghalib was not a swimmer himself, these were his close friends.

Hindus and Muslims both attended the Phoolwalon-ki-Sair, an event meant for fostering communal harmony, with enthusiasm. In October 1847, Emperor Bahadur Shah wrote to the superintendent in charge

[32] *Akhbar-e Rangeen*, p. 62.

[33] *Hayat-e Jawed*, p. 50.

of the fort of his wish to attend the function. In his order he said: 'I desire to visit Phoolwalon-ki-Sair and arrangements should be made for the begums also. It will be appropriate for screens to be erected from Deohri-e Adalat to Lalpurda for the purpose.'[34]

Later, the emperor ordered arrangements to be made to hold Meena Bazaar and for the sons of jewellers from Johri Bazaar to come to help.[35] The upheaval of 1857 threw this entire life out of gear. Ghalib captures the drastic change beautifully:

یا شب کو دیکھتے تھے کہ ہر گوشئہ بساط

دامانِ باغبان و کفِ گل فروش ہے

یا صبح دم جو دیکھیے آکر تو بزم میں

نے وہ سرور و سوز نہ جوش و خروش ہے

At night, every corner was the lap of a garden, the hand of a flower seller

By the morning, there was no trace of pleasure and enthusiasm.

The English sought revenge for 1857. Thousands of the citizens of Delhi became victims of their indiscriminate wrath, ranging from scholars to the unlettered, young to old, durbaris to commoners. A

---

[34] *Ahsan-ul Akhbar*, p. 193.

[35] *Ahsan-ul Akhbar*, p. 193.

benumbed poet, Azurda, could but cry out after the massacre of one of the prominent poets of his time and a close friend, Imam Bakhsh Sahbai:

روز وحشت مجھے صحرا کی طرف لاتی ہے

سر ہے اور جوشِ جنوں سنگ ہے اور چھاتی ہے

ٹکڑے ہوتا ہے جگر جان پر بن جاتی ہے

مصطفےٰ خاں کی ملاقات جو یاد آتی ہے

کیوں نہ آزردہ نکل جائے نہ سودائی ہو

قتل اس طرح سے بے جرم جو صہبائی ہو

Every day, my madness pulls me towards the desert.
There's my head and madness, my chest and stones:
My heart is shattered, my life at its edge
When I recall meetings with Mustafa Khan.
Why shouldn't Azurda be driven to utter madness,
When the innocent Sahbai is murdered?

What else could be the backdrop of this couplet of Ghalib's?

اس رنگ سے اُٹھائی کل اس نے اسدؔ کی نعش

دشمن بھی جس کو دیکھ کے غمناک ہوگئے

The dead body of Asad (Ghalib) was lifted in such a way
Even the eyes of his enemies became wet.

The targeted section of society was the one to which Ghalib was deeply attached. Thinking of comrades who had been put to death he wrote: 'I am swimming in the bloodied waters of this city.'[36] He lamented further: 'I swear

[36] A letter to Chaudary Abdul Ghafoor Surur in September 1860, in Anjum, *Ghalib ke Khutoot*. Some of the letters Ghalib wrote at the time reflect his anguish. In a letter to Anwar-ud Daula Shafaq, penned on 24 August 1860, he wrote, 'Reverend Sir, I am not able to muster up courage to present the account of the devastation and demolition of houses and mosques. I am sure the builder would not have taken such care in building the city as the destroyers have taken for its demolition. The buildings razed to dust mostly inside the qila and some outside it were built by Shahjehan. During the demolition of these buildings, spade after spade was broken. Inside the qila, spades could not serve the purpose of demolition. Tunnels were dug and buildings were dynamited.'

He wrote to Majruh, 'The day before yesterday I rode to visit the wells. It would be no exaggeration to say that I saw a desolate desert sprawling before me from the Jama Masjid to the Raj Ghat gate. If the debris is cleared, an eerie silence will reign supreme.'

In yet another letter to Majruh, he wrote, 'Kashmeeri Katra has been demolished. Now the high gates and big room are no more in sight.'

by Ali that the parting with the dead and the separation with those alive have made my world dark and desolate.'

Delhi's devastation was indeed complete. The city had been ravaged and reconstructed many times before, but this time round, it was not only a destruction of the city: it was as much the end of a civilization, a culture, and a way of life. In a letter written to Mirza Mahdi Majruh on 24 August 1860, Ghalib likened post-1857 Delhi to an uprooted tree.[37] Individuals settle down again after they suffer devastation. But the process of revival of a civilization is never easy. The war in 1857 rendered everyone—kings as well as paupers—helpless and dependent. The devastation gave rise to utter despondency as well as moral degradation and depravity. In a letter to Munshi Hargopal Tafta on 9 April 1861, Ghalib wrote: 'The bitter truth that now dawns is that the begums of the palace go about with faces like that of the waning moon, in untidy dress, crumpled trousers, torn footwear. It is no exaggeration.'[38] It is again Ghalib

---

In a letter to Hussain Mirza, he wrote, 'Buildings for elephants, Falak paira, and Laldiggee, and war fortresses have been demolished.'

In yet another letter to Majruh, he wrote, 'By God, Delhi is no longer a city. It has been turned into a camp.'

[37] Letter of 7 September 1858 in Anjum, *Ghalib ke Khutoot*.

[38] Letter of 9 April 1861, in Anjum, *Ghalib ke Khutoot*.

who said that the women of the qila who had grown old had taken to pimping and the young had become prostitutes.[39]

Ghalib was an eyewitness to the sufferings of Delhi and the violent atrocities it faced. He said: 'This city is no longer a city but a calamity.'[40] What he personally had to endure is evident from his letters. The want of bread made him part with his gown and scarf.[41] During the winter, he was worried about a quilt to keep out the cold.[42] Mansions and diwankhanas lay desolate, houses lay in darkness without light or lamp.[43] Foodgrains were costly and death was cheap.[44] The entire surroundings

[39] Letter to Alaee, 16 February 1862, in Anjum, *Ghalib ke Khutoot.*

[40] Letter of 18 July 1855, in Anjum, *Ghalib ke Khutoot.*

[41] Ghalib wrote to Tafta, 'I had given an imported gown and a scarf, two and a half yards long, to a taut. ... And he came to give me money' (Letter of 18 July 1858, in Anjum, *Ghalib ke Khutoot*).

[42] He wrote to Majruh, 'There is no morsel to eat, no wine to drink. The winter is approaching. I am worried about quilt and mattress' (Letter of October 1858, in Anjum, *Ghalib ke Khutoot*).

[43] He wrote to Tafta, 'No one is left in the city to visit me. House after house is dark, without light' (Letter of 5 December 1857, in Anjum, *Ghalib ke Khutoot*).

[44] He writes to Chaudhary Abdul Ghafur Surur, 'Grain is expensive, death cheap. Grain is being sold at the same rate as fruit' (Letter of September 1860, in Anjum, *Ghalib ke Khutoot*).

were suffocating and Ghalib felt like a man buried alive.
He writes to Yusuf Mirza about this state of mind:

Excessive sorrow makes men go mad, lose their senses, and if
sorrow leads to mental imbalance and loss of my sensibilities,
it should not come as a surprise. It is a surprise only if one
does not grasp this willingly. Ask me about my sorrow—of
death, separation, going hungry, and of loss of dignity.[45]

Cruel circumstances made him run from pillar to
post. His pension was restored after great effort and the
nawab of Rampur eventually fixed a monthly pension of
100 rupees for him; but this was small consolation to a
Ghalib deeply afflicted by suffering. There was grief and
a thousand wounds behind the facade of his smile.

There has been no study of the works of Ghalib from
a historical perspective. Dr Syed Mahmud did attribute
some of Ghalib's verses to the post-1857 period and he
used them to trace his political consciousness and the
impact of the mutiny, but other critics see the same
verses as his poetry of the pre-1857 period. Yet, it is
imperative to analyse Ghalib's poetical works in the
context of contemporaneous events. It would be unfair
to Ghalib to believe that the events and incidents which
befell Delhi and its cultural values did not leave their
mark on his verse. He was a man who was on the verge

[45] Anjum, *Ghalib ke Khutoot*.

of losing all patience following the events, when he wrote:

کیوں گردشِ دوام سے گھبرا نہ جائے دل

انسان ہوں پیالہ و ساغر نہیں ہوں

یا رب زمانہ مجھ کو مٹاتا ہے کس لیے

لوحِ جہاں پہ حرفِ مکرّر نہیں ہوں میں

Why wonder that a life's perpetual cycle should exhaust me fully?
For I am human not inanimate like the goblet holding wine.
Oh God! Why is time so bent upon striking me out
When I am not a word to be writ again on life's slate?

It would be an injustice to Ghalib to believe that he remained unaffected by the cataclysmic events of his time. Maulana Azad correctly pointed out that it was not possible for a person of Ghalib's sensibilities to be a witness to the fateful events without being left broken. Iqbal has, in a letter, extolled an observation of Akbar Ilahabadi's that 'suffering' is a great catalyst for arousing consciousness. The cruelties of time led Ghalib to long for 'incense and shroud' but also sharpened his sensitivities. However, it would be futile to expect from Ghalib commonplace expressions of sorrow. A great thinker or a poet surrenders himself at the altar of life's expediency, but not without great hesitation. In order to understand the matter properly, one has to put Ghalib's state of mind, depth of heart, and philosophical bent together and make a close scrutiny of his 'sensitivity towards sorrows' and 'concern for the honour of sorrows'. For understanding his poetry as a mirror of his emotions, one requires psychological intuition and insight into Ghalib's personality. Ghalib's poetry can be understood only after one is able to develop insights into how 'pain becomes potion'[46] and how the concept of 'the images buried in the earth' can draw one's attention towards 'tulips and flowers'.[47]

A great poet, philosopher, or a reformer does not easily surrender to the odds of life. The body is forced to bend but the spirit remains engaged in struggle. After the mutiny, Sir Syed himself passed an ordeal by fire while reciting the following verse:

حریفِ کاوشِ مژگاں خوں ریزم نۂ ناصح!

بدست آور رگِ جانی و نشتر را تماشا کن

O advisor! You are not aware of the quest of my pupil who drips blood
Put your hand on the jugular vein, and be witness to the sharp lancet on it.

[46] From Ghalib's verses: 'Pain becomes its cure when it crosses its limits.'

[47] Ghalib wrote, 'Not all, but some appeared as tulips and flowers / There are many faces that have disappeared into the earth.'

Ghalib too was tossed around by the turbulent waters,[48] and his suffering, emotions, and sensitivity shaped the contours of his poetry.

[48] From Ghalib's verses: 'Dance like the reflection of a bridge in the waters / Detach your "self" from the body and lose the "self" in whirling space.' According to Anne Marie Schimmel, this couplet reflects the true personality of Ghalib (*Urdu-e Moalla*, Ghalib number, vol. III, p. 104).

Index
....

About the Author and Translator

AUTHOR

K.A. Nizami (1925–1997) was professor of history at the Aligarh Muslim University, India. He was a prolific scholar and wrote extensively in English and Urdu. Some of his well-known writings include *Religion and Politics in India during the 13th Century* (Oxford University Press [OUP], 2002); *On History and Historians of Medieval India* (1983); *Royalty in Medieval India* (1997); and *The Life and Times of Shaikh Nizam-u'd-din Auliya* (OUP, 2007).

TRANSLATOR

Ather Farouqui is the general secretary of Anjuman Taraqqi Urdu (Hind), New Delhi. He is a pioneering scholar of Urdu language and education and has been a recipient of the prestigious Sahitya Akademi Award. He has written his MPhil and PhD dissertations at Jawaharlal Nehru University, New Delhi. His notable publications include the influential essay 'Islamic

Banking in India at the Service of Pan-Islamists'; the play *Marx My Word*; and the edited volumes *Muslims and Media Images: News versus Views* (OUP, 2009) and *Redefining Urdu Politics in India* (OUP, 2006). He has published the English translation of the first archival research book on Bahadur Shah Zafar, *The Life and Poetry of Bahadur Shah Zafar* (2017).